ENGLISH RECUSANT LITERATURE
1558–1640

Selected and Edited by
D. M. ROGERS

Volume 147

P. R.

*The Art
to Dye Well
1626*

P. R.

The Art
to Dye Well
1626

The Scolar Press
1973

ISBN o 85417 962 3

Published and Printed in Great Britain by
The Scolar Press Limited, 20 Main Street,
Menston, Yorkshire, England

NOTE

Reproduced (original size) from the unique copy in the library of the Abbey, Fort Augustus, by permission of the Prior.

Reference: Allison and Rogers 700; not in STC.

THE
ART TO DYE
WELL.

Or a briefe and eafy Methode,
how to direct ones Life, to
a fecure & happy End.

Deuided into three Parts.

By P. R.

For his owne particuler Comfort,
and Profit of fuch, as will
take paynes to vfe it..

In all thy *Works*, remember thy laft *End*,
and thou wilt neuer finne. Ecclef.
7. Verf. 40.

M. DC. XXVI.

THE PREFACE
TO THE
READER.

IF any chance to meruayle why I should now set forth this litle Treatise of the Art to dye well, after so many already printed of of that nature ; I desire them to reflect vpon the variety of mens affections, who are not all alike attracted with one manner of explication of any argument . But the subiect of this discourse being so necessary, and the practice thereof so profitable, and (as I may say`so pleasant, there cāno variety be superfluous , or any new methode

*too tedious : Therefore leauing euery one
to his choyce , among many that I haue
read, this liked me best ; & albeit aswell
for my priuate practice of the language
wherein it was first written in Italian by
a Reuerend spirituall Father , as for the
reformation of my owne life , which I
willingly proposed in this last Holy yeare
of Iubiley, I first tooke the paynes to tran-
slate it into English ; yet I held it a de-
fault to preuent the good of many of my
Nation , who by reading it in English
might be partakers of the same consolatiō
that I my selfe found in the translating of
it, if I should keep it obscure in my owne
priuate scribled papers. For that cause I
haue sent it more legible into the common view by putting it in Print. But I
may be warned by the generall fault of
the world, that some carping humors will
censure me to affect vayne glory, by desiring to see my selfe in print : Such I desire rather to attend to the goodnes of the
matter, then to compose a commentary of
my*

my faults: easily confessing my selfe to haue greater faults, then such a kinde of vayne glory .

Now concerning the translation of the Authour, I am partly ashamed to expresse his Name, for that I haue not altogeather done him true Iustice, partly by deforming , in my rude Phrase , his pure Eloquence in so polite a language; partly by leauing out many of his Chapters , which albeit they were excellent good of themselues, yet I held them not so necessary for my intended purpose to procure more customers to reade a little , who might be tyred to reade twice as much . Wherein I hope my open confession may merit pardon for this my boldnes, & preoccupate the accusation of my Aduersaries .

As for the argument which treateth of a dayly preparation for our last Conclusion, I cannot choose but much deplore the cowardly spirit of such Christians, as hold it a melancholy action continually to meditate on their death : since they must needes

A 3

needes confesse nothing to be more certayne, considering the Scripture doth af-
sure vs, There is no man who liueth, but must dye : nothing more
necessary, which Christ proued by the
grayne of corne, that vnlesse it were first
dissolued into corruption. it could not
yield new, and more ample fruite; nothing more profitable, that by our naturall death, this corruptible matter should
be conuerted into incorruptibility, and
our mortall body be inuested with immortality; no hing so pleasant, as that
the miseryes of this world should be exchanged for e ernall ioyes & glory.

This could the very Pagans easily vnderstand, who hearing the Philosopher
Plato to reade, dispute, or write of the
Immortality of the soule, became so raui-
shed with the eager desire to atteyne therunto, as many did contemne their present liues, and killed themselues; so as the
Philosophers were compelled by the Na-
tionall Lawes to desist from reading of
that

that *subiect* any more. Is it not a great shame then, for vs to see the Heathens, who had no conceyte of any other increase of glory, but only of a perpetuity of being, should offer violence vnto themselues; and we who are taught by the Holy Ghost, that this present life is lent vs for no other cause, but to prepare a passage to the fruition of eternall glory, in the vision of Almighty God, that we should be so dull, as not euery houre to desire to meditate on that, without the which we neuer will be able to attayne vnto the other? And as the common Lawes prohibited the Philosophers proceeding any further in that argument; so certainely our sinnes, and guilty conscience is the only obstruction of our willing consideration of death.

The Poet could affirme, the feare death to be worse then death; but a Christian ought to thinke, and will find true by experience, that a dayly preparation for our death, will mitigate the horrour,

A 4   and

and *paynes of death it selfe*. *We dayly
see that common Souldiers who fight but
for base profit*, *or opinion of Honour, at
first entring into the field, are easily affrighted*, *and will runne away: but after they haue beene compelled by their
Captaynes to returne*, *and indure the
battell hauing thereby once obtayned victory of their enemy, wil neuer after feare
any dangers*, *but couragiously behaue
themselues: Euen so a Christian Sou-
lier who maketh warre for an ineſtimable reward of eternall glory by many
light skirmishes with death in his life,
will easily contemne the grisly Vizarde,
which the feare of death apprehendeth.
But howsoeuer we striue to shunne
Death, yet Death will not fayle to follow and ouertake vs*, *and the more vn-
prouided he findeth vs to expect him*, *the
more hideous he appeareth vnto vs*. Oh
Death, how bitter art thou to a mã
that putteth his confidence in his
worldly riches! *But he who aspireth
after*

after the ioyes of heauen, will cry earnestly, I desire to be dissolued, and
with Christ.

And since from the first houre that we
come into the world, we presently receaue
the sentence of death irreuocable, and
that euery day we seeme to liue, is but a
lingering progresse vnto the execution of
that sentence, whether we will or no;
Let vs (as soone as we inioy the vse of
Reason) ayde our selues therewith, so as
we may make a fit preparation warily to
walke in the feare of offending of God;
who beholding our humility in voluntary
offering vp our transitory liues vnto his
pleasure, he will mercifully leade vs
through the strait gate of Death, into his
spatious Pallace of endles Ioyes; whither that I may the better ariue, I humbly craue all their good prayers, who
shall happen to read this booke.

A 5

The

The first part of the *Arte to dye well*; wherin is handled that mãner of preparatiõ which a man in his best health, should make to purchase a happy end.

Of the Breuity of mans life.
Chap. 1.

SHORT are the dayes of man vpon earth, as ordi-nary experiéce teacheth, and yet men flatter them selues, that they may liue long. The reason is, becaufe they are willing to belieue that which they fee not, and, should not belieue; but are loath to affent to that, which is

most

most certaine. This is one of the greatest errours in the world, and ariseth from the disorderly affectiō man beareth to himself. For from an inordinate desire to liue, must needes arise a great auersion from death. For that he expoundeth death to depriue him violently of that which he most cordially affecteth. For which cause, man doth not only seeke with all diligence to auoide the actuall separation of this present life, but laboreth to remoue from his cogitation the very conceit of death: and is loath, that should fall vpon him, wherunto his desire inclineth him not.

This is a great infirmity, that afflicteth generally al the ofspring of *Adam*, but most especially the Grandies of this world. The reason is, for that they reposing their greatest consolation in this present life, the very cogitation of death, repre-

A 6   senteth

senteth vnto them an infinite defo-
lation. But who is there that may
not eafily difcerne, that it is a moft
vaine cogitation, to feeke to expell
the confideratiõ of death? for death
forbeareth neuer the more to fteale
vpon vs, becaufe we determine not
to thinke of him. Surely it would
proue the wifer way, to runne a
cleane contrary courfe. That fince
our prefent life vanifheth like a
fhadow, and death maketh haft to
furprize vs, let vs make as greate
haft to confider, what preparation
will be fitteft for that foden paffage: after which, either perpetuall
life, or eternall death, muft follow
of neceffity.

    In this preparation doth confift
the Iuftice, Prudence, Temperáce,
and Fortitude of a Chriftian. And
if euer from the firft creation of the
worlde it hath bene the Counfell
of the fupremeft Wifedome, that
             we

we should thinke attentiuely vpon
our last passage out of this life , it
easily may appeare much more necessary in this age we liue in , for
that mans life appeareth sensibly
to be continually abreuiated ; that
in cōparison to the age of our pre-
decessours, in these tymes our birth
and death may seeme as ioyned together , as *Iob cap.* 10. expressed in
this wordes : *Thy handes haue made
me, and framed euery part, and so on a
soden thou ouerthrowest me.* Intending,
God had no sooner perfected all
our parts , but immediatly he doth
ruinate, and vndoe them againe.

And the same *Iob cap.* 9. vseth
this demonstration : *As an Ægle taking his flight to get his prey,* meaning
to expresse the greatest celerity that
may be . And it may well appeare
that the Patriarch *Iacob* had the
same sensible feeling of this present
life, when he trauailed into Ægipt

to

to fee his beft beloued fonne *Iofeph*;
who being brought to the preten-
ce of *Pharao* , and being queftioned
by the King of his age, he anfwe-
red : *The dayes of the pilgrimage of my
life are few , & ill , & are not come nigh
the age of my fore-fathers.* Gen 44. Behold two witneffes without exception, vnto whom in that time the
dayes of their life appeared very
fhort, and they both haue confeffed
it fo playne.

Notwithftandinge in thefe our
dayes , when we come as fhort to
the years of thefe two, as they atteined to the age of their fore-fathers,
men thinke they are priuiledged,
as if they had made fome conuenát
with death, and Hell. But I apprehend not what anfwere the Lords
of this world (who are blinded
with this errour) will make here-
vnto. That albeit their haire is turned all white, and they be decaied
                                    much

much in ftrength , which are moft
certaine meffengers of death at
hand : yet will they not giue credit
to that which they fee , and feele
but fondly feeding their imagina-
tions with vaine hopes , or deceaued by Aftrologers , contrary to
Gods Commandement, and inclining to their owne defires , they
will hardly be induced to belieue
their life will be fhort. It were better that the Princes of this world
fhould be very attentiue vnto this
point , and in their old age to refraine to do the actions of yonge
men, which will afford fmall confolation vnto them , who fhould
meditate on their death.

For what comfort can Chriftiã
piety receyue , in building of new
and fumptuous pallaces , for him,
who by al likelyhood cannot liue
aboue foure or fiue yeares ? What
thinke you would thefe men doe,
if

if they might prolonge their dayes
to nine hundred and thirty yeares
as *Adam*? or to nine hundred threescore and nine, as *Mathufalem* did?
What new towers of *Babell* would
they fall a building, to make their
aboade eternall in this world, if
they could? Oh incredulity of the
louers of the world! This day dieth
a yonge man of twenty yeares, that
in ability seemed he might haue liued to be an old man: yesterday
departed a youth of twelue yeares, that then did but enter to taft
of the delightes of the world. And
yet a man of threescore, that feeleth
his spirit wasteth, his strength de-
caieth, and that his fire is euen consumed to afhes, doth labour notwithftandinge to finde out some
strange deuice, to prolonge his
yeares infinitely. And will by no
meanes yield to belieue, that he
shall be sodenly called to make his
ac-

accompt. And be violently separated from that life , which so disorderly he loued . Wherfore I will conclude this Chapter, desiring the Reader like a good Christian , to thinke that his longest life will be but short . Because this cogitation will much profit his soule, not only in this life , but also in the life that will endure for euer.

Of what importance it is to die well.

Chap . 2 .

IF all the Orators in the world, if all the writers of bookes, if all they who haue any speciall guift , or skill to teach any Art , or Science, and who in this world are adored for their wits, should straine all their vaynes, & extend all their wits ; all they , are not sufficient to expresse, or iustly to ponder, how much it behooueth one single man

to

to make a happy conclufion of his
life. The reafon is euident. For being not able to conceaue the nature of Eternity after death, how
fhould they proportion the importance of that moment, on which
dependeth eternal, eyther life, or
death? yet the bright light of Chrift
Iefus fayth, that hath reftored new
fight to the blinded children of *A-*
dam, is of its one nature fufficient
for Chriftians, to forme in their
vnderftandinge a certayne notion
of the perfect excellency of dying
well. Which may ferue them to
the right vfe to preferue their liues
by the affiftance of God his grace
in good ftate, to perfect their end.
And for this reafon, thofe few that
treade the path of the narrow way
that leadeth to eternall life, hold
alwaies an attentiue care of the end
of their iourney.

For albeit moft commonly they
liue

liue pioufly, yet dare they neuer
reft affured; but they tremble like
the Apfen-tree leaues when any
wind bloweth , reteyning ftill in
their harts not a feruile, but a filiall
feare, of loofing that which they
hope to gayne. For who knoweth
how he may dye ? Who can promife himfelfe that moft pretious
Iewell , the guift of perfeuerance ? And there is no caufe to
wonder, that the Iuft , for the
prefent time, haue continually, not
anxiety, but this carefull diligence,
and know how to prize the ineftimable valour of a good death .
They are fure, that to dye well,
is a certayne condition annexed,
for man to receiue the eternall reward which they haue labored to
deferue, with their great and tedious afflictions in this life . Whereas
on the contrary, diuers who haue
begun excellently well , as *Iudas*
among

among Chrift his owne elected A-
poftles, made a moft defperate end.
And *Saul* in the beginning of his
Reygne liued free of reprehenfion,
but his latter end was not anfwe-
rable to his beginning . Wherefore
Iuftice at one tyme will not ferue,
if it be not confummated with a
like death .

And therefore the Iuft, with
fighes from the bottome of their
hart, do euer crye to God , mercy-
fully to beftow on them his moft
gracious guift of dying well . Re-
ueretly fearing their owne frailty,
leaft by their owne falt they may
be forfaken of Gods grace . They
know alfo, that a good death of a
Chriftian (being confidered only in
its one nature , for no other caufe,
but for what fenfe the foule feeleth
in that agony) is worthy of infinite eftimation . For euen in that
houre, when all the wit, ftrength,

riches forſake man, the mercy of
God doth ſo comfort the hart of a
good man, that it ouercometh all
the paynes of death it ſelfe, the
feare of hell, and the terrour of the
rigorous iuſt iudgement of God.
And at what tyme the proude
Princes of the earth ſhall faint, and
tremble for feare, the Good man
will confidently preſent himſelfe
before his Creatour, being infinit-
ly comforted by the teſtification of
his innocency, & by a firme hope
of eternal reward from God.

This certainly is an admirable
comfort, and more to be affected
then all the Principalityes or vaine
pleaſures of the world, although
the world ſhould endure a húdred
Millions of ages. And this deſire by
a naturall inſtinct is in al men. For
there is not any, liue he neuer ſo
badly, but deſireth to dye well,
as *Balaam* well demonſtrated,
                                    who

who being wicked himselfe, yet he prayſed the people of God in deſpite of the King of *Moab*, ſaying: *God graunt I may dye as theſe Iuſt, and my end be like vnto theirs. Num. 23.* He beheld (as he ſtood) the campe of the Iſraelites, among whome there were many iuſt, whoſe death Prophetically he foreſaw, and he deſired to be partaker of the felicity they would ariue vnto at their death, although he would not imitate their beginning, to wit, their deuout liuing. And ſo depriuing himſelfe willingly of the firſt, he was agaynſt his will iuſtly debarred of the laſt.

This errour is crept in among moſt Chriſtians, who vnderſtanding, by the fayth they doe profeſſe, the infinite happynes of thoſe who dye in the Grace and fauour of God, they wiſh to dye as good men do, but they ſpend their life ſo

far

far different from the others, as I
fee no likelyhood, how they fhold
obtayne their other earneſt, but
vayne defire. For the gate of life is
neuer opened vnto them, who
(while time is graunted vnto them
to do fuch actions as might deme-
rit euerlaſting life) giue themſelues
ouer as vanquiſhed, vnto the deceitfull pleaſures and bewitching
paſtimes of the world. But it is alwayes fet wide open for fuch, as
know how to value, and carefully
to negotiato in this life for the laſt
houre of death. They who moile
& toile heare in this life, ſhall haue
eaſe graunted them in the houre of
death. According vnto the words
of *S. Iohn* in the Apocalyps: *Bleſſed*
are they who dye in our Lord: Now
commandeth the ſpirit, that they reſt
from their labours. This ſaying is of
great comfort to the Iuſt that dye,
and ſerueth for a ſingular leſſon for
those

those that liue. Because it proposeth
a most blessed end of their labours,
proclayming thē blessed that shall
dye well, and also pointeth out the
path which leadeth to that end,
which is labour, and care, and
workes of piety, for which in the
eueninge of the day they expect
their earnest penny of euerlasting
life, proposed to the labourers in
our Lords vineyard.

The first Precept of dying well, is conti-
nually to thinke of Death. Chap. 3.

IT being confessed that our life
is so short, as in the first chapter
I haue declared, and the commodity of dynge well truly prised, as in
the second Chapter; I will now
begin to set downe in order certaine precepts of this Art, that by helpe of a good methode, the reader
may the easier imprint the same in
his

his mind. Wherefore the first precept is, the continuall cogitation of death, not such a deliberate and fixed cogitation, as a holy Queene of Spaine had, who alwayes appointed one of her Ladies who attended her, to performe her charge at all Festiuities, to whisper in her eare, Your Maiesty may be pleased to remember, that on necessity you must dye: but an ordinary, and quiet memoriall, as may helpe towards a spirituall direction of our life.

For euen as a man who traueleth a long iourney, by often thinking on the end thereof, disposeth carefully to keepe the direct passages that may best conduct him thither: euen so a mans often remembrance of his death, helpeth him to order his life piously, as continuall experience maketh most certaine: Wheras the obliuion of death causeth

B seth

seth worldly mé to grow insolent, like fat wild Bulls to run flinginge through the fieldes of sensuall delightes of this deceitfull world: as if they should neuer be led perforce vnto the place of execution of the Iustice of Almighty God. But contrarywise the liuely representation of our death, doth mortify the immoderate apetites of the vanities of this world, and tempers the violence of our passions by a forcible & admirable meanes. And for this cause, the Spouse of Christ his holy Catholike Church, gouerned by the spirit of God, at the beginninge of Lent, in those dayes that are ordeined to admonish all to reforme their liues, putteth them in mind of the necessary memory of their death, by that most significant ceremony of giuing of ashes, & with those wordes which God him selfe pronounced vnto Adam

after

after he had transgressed his command; *Dust thou art, and into dust thou shalt returne againe. Gen. 3.*

This cogitation maketh a man looke home vpon his mold of clay, least he grow prowd and insolent ouer his neighbour. This thought cooleth the heat of the flesh, that it rage not furiously after sensual apetites. This recordation quieteth the insatiable famine after riches, by expressing how needles they are for him that must very quickly forsake them. Hereupon diuers holy men, for feare they might to longe forget so necessary and profitable a consideration, introduced first the practise to tye some hard corde about them, or to set before them in their Oratory the scull of some dead man, with intent to awake their drowsy memory, and to quicken their spirit, temperatly to spend this short life, and carefully to trafike for

the

the riches of a better future life. Yet concerning thefe exercifes a man muft be carefull, leaft (if the foule doe not vfe fome prudency) they may before they obferue it, loofe the profit by abufe, or for want of fome skilfull fpirituall guide.

For as we obferue how it fuc-ceedeth in diuers Hofpitals, where they beinge fo ordinarily accufto-med to fee men dye, and do not carefully confider the circuftances that accompany that finall paffage, after a while they loofe that pious fenfe of death, and they ftand ga-zing without eyther feare of their own, or comiferation of them who dye before them: So likewife may it happen vnto fome fpiritual per-fons, who keeping a dead mans head in their chambers, after they haue vfed to looke often vpon it, without due application of it to the felues, they become as forgetful

by

by negligéce of their owne death,
as if that memorial had no relation
vnto them. And by this experience
I would thinke it more profitable
for euery particular man to keepe
such a head in some priuate place
where they come seldome, vnlesse
they retire themselues to exercise
some act of deuotion, when they
may vse it as a helpe to stir vp their
meditation by due consideration
of the obiect. I sayd for euery particular man, because to mooue a
whole community I hold it more
conuenient that such pious memo-
rialls should be set out in publick,
to moue them in generall, where
euery priuat person hath not conueniency of a priuate Oratory.

But albeit this kinde of motiue
be good, yet I thinke it will be
more effectuall, to goe sometimes
to assist those who lye a dyinge,
with intent to behold them, and

imagine it your own cafe, & what variety of accidents vfe to happen in that houre; becaufe this true and reall death (not a figure, or painted death) will moue a man ftrongly to liue deuoutly; and that impreffion vfeth to ftick by one for many dayes, and produceth a greater effect, then the hearinge of many a fermon, or reading ouer in haft diuers fpirituall bookes.

And from this it is proued what compunction and emulation the pious death of fome good religious mā in the reformed Cloifters doth vfe to moue to the whole Couent, who vfe to affift the dying man; that for diuers dayes after, there appeareth an extraordinary ftricte reformation through the whole Cloifter, as if euery particular had his part in that dying man. Which example preferueth them from many daungers of temptations, and

nota-

notably incourageth their spirits.
The sight of this dying man maketh all the Religious more fearefull of their owne frailties, more silent, more modest, more recolle-
cted, more diligent of obseruing
their vowes, like men who do expect euery houre to be called to
render a most strict account of all
their actions, and expect to receiue
(they dare not presume which) either perpetuall reward, or eternall
punishmét from the iustice of God.

The second precept is, to liue in this life
conuersing in the sight of God as before
a most strict iudge, so that at our death
we may finde him a most louing Fa-
ther. Chap. 4.

Since it is most certaine that the
feare of death in a Christian, is
not so terrible for that it depriueth
him of life, as for the accompt he is

to

to render after his Death; Reason
therfor would that in our life time
we should be prepared alwayes for
the reckoning we muſt make after
we are departed out of this world.
And our preparation is nothing els
but ſo to order our ſelus in this life,
as if we were preſently to appeare
before the Iudgement of Almighty
God. For this is the common intention of all thoſe, that accuſtome
them ſelues diligently to be ready
for that houre. Therfore the ſecond
precept of this Art ſhall be, to liue
ſo heare in the ſight of God, as here-
after we would appeare before his
rigorous Iuſtice, that doth obſerue
and number, not only all our actions, but euery cogitation, to demaund an accompt thereof.

　　And it may well appeare, that
this counſell is very neceſſary. For
becauſe he who liueth with this
ſtrictnes, diſpoſeth all his actions
with

with a perpetual regard what must
needs follow in the iustice of God:
therefore he vseth great circumspection to preuent his condemna-
tion before that seuere Tribunall.
He will not trust the approbation
of men, who many tymes will al-
low of that, which in the iudgement of God will be faulty, and he
doth as it were preuēt God (wherwith God is highly pleased) by cō-
demning himselfe. By which religious policy he is much vnbur-
dened of the weight of his sinnes,
which otherwise being negligently left vnto Gods enquiry, must
needs haue byn most seuerely cen-
sured: Since God hath pleased to
promise, that he, who truly heere
shall iudge himselfe, shall neuer a-
gayne for those offences be iudged
by him as guilty.

This Counsell haueall (whom
the Church of God recounteth for
B 5   Saints)

Saints) most strictly obserued, as
we read in their liues. So we read
of that Holy and learned Father S.
Hierome, that he practised so rigorous discipline on himselfe, as may
seeme in their apprehension (who
know not how to weigh the actiõs
of holy men) to haue byn too violent. So likewise we read of S.
Onuphrius, Sonne to the King of
Persia, and of S. *Antony*, and infinite
more, who haue voluntarily in-
flicted such punishment on their
sinnes, which they well conside-
red had caused our Sauionr to endure so cruel tormẽts for their sake,
as may mooue horrour to such as
read their liues. But it is no meruayle if these holy men of the new
Testament (reading dayly in the
Gospell, of the horrour of death, &
the rigour of Gods Iustice) did desire both, to conforme themselues
vnto his loue, & to make some conuenient

uenient satisfaction for their sinns.
As before in the old law that holy man *Iob*, being canonized for a
perfect Saint by the mouth of God,
conuersed in this world with God
as with a most rigorous iudge ,
who watched narrowly all the
workes he did, and would not o-
uersee one fault vnpunished *Iob. 9.*
Thus *Iob* meant by these wordes :
*I feared euery one of my deedes, knowing
thou wouldest not spare me, if I offended
thee.* And if any desire to marke vnto what degree of feare this most
true friend of God atteined, he will
expresse himselfe in these wordes :
*I feared God as the swelling waues that
seemed to come rowling ouer mee , the
weight whereof I was not able to beare.
Iob. 31.* This was the meaning *Iob* ,
whose testimony is most certayne
and whose example only is sufficient, without producing many.

But he that thus liueth before
B 6   the

the fight of God, and will not rely
on the opinions of men, at the end
of his life fhall certainly find, how
the mercy of God will neuer fayle
him : as often hath beene tryed
in the deaths of fundry holy men ,
who after this methode haue cary-
ed themfelues, enioying not one
day of eafe, nor as a man may fay,
not once beholding the cleare and
mild countenance of their God,
but in tribulations and feare of reprobation ; in the ending of their
life haue enioyed a moft admirable
quiet of their foule . The diuine Iuftice taking off his hard hand of
correction,and cherifhing vp their
long fufteyned forrowes for their
finnes, with vnfpeakable mercyes,
and internall confolation . The
which hath byn outwardly euidēt
vnto the beholders of the death of
fuch holy men, who fome daies before their departure out of their life,
haue

haue demonftrated in their countenance, wordes, and actions fuch
a tranquility, comfort, and fecuri-
ty of the infinite bounty & fweetnes of God, who feemed to attract
them vnto him , as deferuing to be
partners with him in his eternall
glory; who were contented in this
life to drinke of the cup of his bitter
Paffion with him in conformity of
his loue, giuing them heere before
their death , a taft of their future
ioyes , and leauing to others a ioyfull fpectacle to encourage them
ftoutly to treade thofe pathes that
they vfed to walke in .

The third Precept is , to take fpeciall care
neuer to commit any mortall finne,
for feare leaft death furprife vs in fo
dangerous an eftate. Chap. 5.

THis precept is the moft principall, and of neceffity, that
can

can be giuen or thoght on by him,
who purposeth to dye well. For
the perpetuall care, not to be in
such a state (as man knoweth according to the Iustice or God doth
deserue eternall damnation) will
be vnto him a good caution to dye
in the peace & fauour of God. The
conueniency of this precept is vnderstood by the nature of mortall
sinne, which causeth a man to be
out of the fauour of his Creatour.
In so much as if Christiãs did beare
but so much loue to their own bodyes and soules as they should, by
this precept they would learne to
liue more warily, and feare God
more then they do.

And to tell you what I thinke,
it seemeth to me a very strange
matter, that whereas euery simple
man doth know, that from the very first instant that one giueth consent to mortall sinne, he remaineth

pre-

prefently guilty of eternall damnation and feparation from God ;
not only the fimple man but alfo
many that are worldly wife , doe
not only offend in confent, but cōmit many foule & horrible crimes:
and yet they eate, fleep, and laugh,
as if they fhould neuer come in the
hands of God to be iudged by him.
But I requeft the Reader of this , if
he haue a defire to dye well , that
he wil (to help him to obferue this
precept) enter into confideration
of the ftate of thofe who are out of
Gods fauour. Becaufe this confideration will be a good meanes to
preferue him from mortall finne, as
the loathfomnes of fickenes caufeth thofe who loue to liue at eafe ,
to feeke to procure preferuatiues of
their health.

They who are out of Gods fauour , cannot choofe but graunt,
that foden death may afwell fall on
them-

themselues, as on others : and yet
they doe not prouide to refrayne
from the prouocations of mortall
sinne, at least for the loue of their
own body, for whose respect they
sinne so often. I wonder, that their
hart trembleth not at euery rumour
of another mans death, imagining
the ministers of Gods iustice, may
come to take hold of themselues,
and hale them violently to the fire
of Hell. They find by familiar
examples, when a Traytour to an
earthly King, to auoyd the Iustice
of his countrey flyeth into far coun-
treyes, when he thinketh himselfe
most secure, eyther by the remote-
nes of the place, or for any guard he
keepeth about his person : yet doth
the guiltines of his own cōscience,
or feare of due punishment, so torment his minde, as he can hardly
enioy any quiet rest.

Can then any man that hath
mali-

malitiousiy offended the King of
Heauen, his God, his Creatour,
his Iudge, from whose power
none can escape, nor fly out of his
iurisdiction; can there any man,
I say, liue without feare of his Iustice? Certainely there is nothing
to be answered in such a case, but
that the Diuell hath too great power ouer that soule, to deteyne it
in extreme blindnes, and infernall
stupidity. *Cain* was a wicked man
and of a hard hart, yet for all that
as soone as he vnderstood Gods
curse, & that he was banished from
the presence of his God for the mur-
ther of his innocent brother *Abel*,
he could not dissemble the intollerable feare that surprised him, but
expressed it in these wordes: *Behold
thou doest this day cast me forth from the
face of the earth and from thy face I shall
be excluded. I must wander like a Rogue
about the earth, whosoeuer findeth me wil
kill*

kill me. Gen. 4.

These were the words of *Cain*.
Out of which I will deduce this
consequence, which although it
serued not him, yet it may, & ought
to serue others to good purpose,
making this argument. I am driuen
out of that land which I possessed
quietly (before I committed this
sinne) vnder thy protection, but
now I am driuen out, *and forced to
runne vp and downe like a Vagabond*.
This Antecedent is grounded on
the displeasure of God, frō whence
ariseth this Consequence, *Therefore
any that findeth me, may kill me:* As if in
other wordes he had sayd, I shall e-
uer liue in feare, and not be able to
take any quiet rest, whiles I am out
of thy fauour : & since all thy creatures are ministers of thy Iustice, I
may well gesse, they will all reuenge the Iniuryes done to thee,
and set on me, and kill me. Wherefore

fore I shall no sooner see any man come towardes me, but I shall thinke that in good reason he commeth to execute on me the Iustice belonging vnto thee.

This was the true sense of *Cains* words, who albeit he were so hard harted, and blinded in soule when he killed his innocent Brother; yet after, the testimony of his owne iniustice, and the euidence of the Iustice of God, did force his vnderstanding iustly to feare the punishment of that fact, which before he should haue feared to haue comitted. But from hence doth most certainly follow, that such Christians, who drowse in such a false security, knowing they haue committed mortall sinne, and do not prouide to rise out of the same in time; they are more blind and dull then *Cain*, & are most like to fall into the Iustice of God, before they open their eyes,

eyes . For which caufe I earneftly
defire all thofe who meane to dye
well , to haue a fpeciall care not to
fall into fo vnhappy an eftate , as
aduifedly to be in the disfauour of
Almighty God . But to liue with
that attention, keeping a watch o-
uer themfelues , and carefully pre-
feruing the ineftimable treafure of
Gods fauour .

The fourth Precept is, fuddenly to rife out
of mortall finne by the Sacrament of
Pennance, to the end that death may
find vs in good eftate. Chap. 6.

THERE is no man fo great
an enemy to himfelfe, that hauing receyued a mortall wound,
but feeketh remedy with all poffible fpeed . Neyther is it neceffary
to prooue this by example , fince
they , who tender their owne life,
are not only diligent to get al help
for

for a deadly wound, but are curious
to seeke remedy for the sleightest
hurt that they haue . Wherefore he
that shall obserue the ouer much
care that men take to preserue this
miserable life , and the extreme
negligence that is vsed to auoyd
the eternall death of the soule and
body, may be much amazed, how
so perilous negligence can remaine
in the mind of a Christian , and so
vnfit for a Catholike man. Certainly they who feare God , and desire
to dye well , whensoeuer they slip
into any mortall sinne , eyther by
violence of temptation, or by frailty, or by negligent ignorance, they
will not let one houre passe, before
they will repent it , with purpose
to confesse, and returne by meanes
of the Sacrament of Pennance into
the fauour of God.

This doctrine is proper vnto the
elect, vnto whome it hapneth that
they

they fall into some sinne, as the
Sonnes of *Adam* : But they no sooner perceiue they are stroken by
the old serpent, but presently they
fly for help vnto the fountayne, I
meane the Sacraments, which are
conduits or pipes that do lead vnto
vs the salutiferous Bloud of our
Sauiour, to purify vs from our sin,
& which reuest vs with the wedding garment of grace, that we had
cast off. Or els they retyre themselues, and with great bitternes of
true contrition, do lament for hauing committed the sinne, which is
so offensiue vnto God ; euen as S.
Peter did, who hauing receyued a
wound, eyther by the sleight of the
Diuell, or by his owne infirmity,
denying Christ to be his mayster,
so soone as he had perfected that
sinne, what did he? The Euange-
list *Saint Luke* will tell you: *He went
forth from the place, & most bitterly wept
for*

for his offence. Luc. 22. In which
wordes, we muſt obſerue, that firſt
he went forth of that place, that
miniſtred temptation vnto him: &
after he bewayled his great offence
agaynſt his mayſter. Theſe words
may inſtruct others that deſire to
returne to the grace of God, which
they haue negligently caſt off, firſt
to ſeparate théſelues from the prouocations & allurements of ſinne,
if they deſire to perfect the act of
true contrition, wherby they may
truly be reconciled vnto the fauor
of God .

I remember that I ſayd before,
that this doctrine of preſent recon-
ciliatiõ of ones ſelfe vnto the mercy of God, was peculiar and proper
vnto thoſe that are elected, eyther
by the Sacrament of Pennance, or
by true contrition. But I meant not
ſo to deuide thoſe two meanes, as if
I would affirme, that a man can reconcile

concile himselfe to Gods fauour by
any contrition neuer so great, if he
will voluntarily neglect the Sacrament of Pennance, if eyther actually he may repayre vnto it, or at
least doth not hartily desire to perfect his contrition by the Sacramét
of Pennance, which ordinarily
C H R I T hath appointed in his
Church. But because it may fall out
so ill, as in tyme of persecution, or
some other suddayne necessity, that
a man cannot alwayes haue oportu-
tunity of a Confessour, or may be
hindred by any serious businesse,
to haue present recourse to the Sacrament it selfe : in such a case, let
him make a solide act of Contrition in his hart, with determination
to confesse at his oportunity. By
this, I say, he that hath aliened himselfe from Gods grace by mortall
sinne, may recouer his fauour a
new. And it may be, that by execution

cution of this Counsell, a seruant of God may commit two hundred mortall sinnes in one yeare, and neuer be two hundred houres seuered from the fauour of God.

This therfore may be a great comfort against many accidents that happen vnlooked for. Yet for all this, because it is not an easy matter to make a perfect act of cōtrition when we would, they who feare God reuerently, for all that they vse their diligence after the example of *S. Peter* retiring frō occasions, & sorrowing for their transgressions, yet dare they not ouer trust their owne griefe, but will make all hast they can to the most sure remedy, which is the vse of the Sacrament, interrupting all temporall impediments to come neere vnto God ; neglecting the wordes and censures of men, to relye only on the true iudgement

C of

of God. As S. *Mary Magdalen* did,
who (although she knew that
Christ was inuited to the house of
a Pharisee) finding her selfe wounded with sinne, and earnestly see-
kinge remedy, not standinge on
wordly cerimonyes, to presse into
another mans house, but at that
time, and very houre, when most
men forget God, & their own conscience, she searched & found out
Christ, with a most cordiall repentance, and obteined a perfect remission of all her sinnes at the handes
of our most high Priest I E S V S
C H R I S T. Who approued well
the hast she made, & the freedome
of her mind, to seeke out the mercy of God, reiectinge all humane
respects.

That act of S. *Magdalen* (offered
vnto her hart by the grace of the
holy Ghost) in the iudgement of
the wysemen of the world might
                              seeme

seeme reprehéſible, but in the ſight of God, it was ſo approued, that he commaunded that deede of hers ſhould be recorded, and preached vnto the end of the world, to controle the preſuminge wiſedome of thoſe, who doate on the vanities of the world. Now therfore let the Reader chooſe whoſe opinion he liketh beſt . But if he deſire to take the ſecureſt, I preſume he had rather reſolue not to ſleepe one night in a conſcience, guilty of one mortall ſinne, like vnto thoſe fooliſh Virgins , vnto whome the ſpouſe ſayed, I know you not: but that he will haſten to bath himſelf with the warme blood of Chriſt, which is found in the Sacrament of Pennance.

The fifth precept is, carefully to conserue,
and increase Gods grace, that we may
find courage and strength in the com-
bat of our last houre. Chap. 7.

CErtainely the diligence is admirable of such, who enter
the lists to fight a combate, both to
prepare and vse such weapons and
armour, by which, and with their
owne nimblenes, they may not
only defend them selues, but also
hope to vanquish their aduersary,
and to increase their one honour.
And surely the curiosity that some
principal persons in our dayes haue
expressed in the like actions, hath
byn so exquisite (although it hath
byn performed with small edification, if not rather with great scan-
dall of their neighbors) that to be
reported might seeme incredible,
if it had not bene confirmed by diuers

ners eye witneſſes. But this art of theſe vnfortunate Adorers of the vanities of the world, ought to be a wholeſome document for thoſe who deſire to dye well: Knowing that at that houre he muſt of force enter the liſts, and fight a combat in a cruell battel with ſuch power-full enemyes, and in ſuch an aduantagious time againſt himſelfe, as the enemy will not omit: Wherin he can make vſe of no other weapon or armour, but the grace of God, and his owne willing cooperation therewith, to vanquiſh his malitious foe, and obtayne that conqueſt which euery Chriſtiā ſhould pretend.

This is a matter of great importance not well vnderſtood & conſidered by euery Chriſtian, who know not how to pōder the great peril of an euil death, and the great power of Gods grace. But they are

C 3   cons

contented if they finde themselues
free from mortall sinne, and if they
haue at any time committed any,
they haue confessed the same after
an ordinary manner, without casting further for the time to come.
Surely, our Sauiour Christ may
well complaine of such vnproui-
dent men, for that hauing left them
so many meanes, wherewith they
might (had they byn diligent) prouided necessary store agaynst that
hower, they liue so carelesly that
they neuer seeme to thinke of the
eternall life. For it seemeth they
care for no more, but what is pre-
cisely of necessity to be quitted of
mortall sinne, and then they thinke
themselues in state good inough if
they so dye: litle thinking that the
most valiant Soldiers doe in that
passage encounter with horrible
combats, and that with great difficulty the Iust is saued. Yet these
who

who hardly may be called Iust,
paſſe on with a bold confidence,
which I know not how it will
ſucceed with them.

Oh what ods is there to iudge of
death a farre of, or cloſe at hand! S.
Hilarion was none of thoſe, who
had prouided not ſcantly, but abõ-
dance of all ſortes of vertues, not-
withſtanding when he grew cloſe
to the gate of death, he found himſelfe ſurpriſed with ſo vnexpected
an aſſault of feare, as vnto his owne
hart, ſeeming to retire for feare of
death, he was conſtreined to ſay
theſe wordes worthy of eternall
memory: Goe forth my ſoule, what
art thou afraid? take hart, goe confidently out of my body; Theſe
threeſcore and ten yeare thou haſt
ſerued our Lord, & doſt thou now
feare death? If this holy Abbot was
faine to vſe theſe wordes, who all
his life time ſtudied to arme him-
              C 4   ſelfe

felfe with liuely courage againſt
the houre of his death, and yet it
ſeemed he felt need to ſtir vp new
courage in himfelfe with that dou-
bling, Goe forth , Goe forth my
foule, that he might the better reſiſt the terrour of death and horrour of Gods ſeuere Iudgement:
Then what wil theſe iuſt men fay,
that neuer arme themfelues againſt
that houre, when they ſhall finde
themfelues brought into ſo great a
ſtiaite?

But I pray God that ſome of thē
find not themfelues much begui-
led. For if their iuſtice (which they
prefume to be fufficient) be no ſtrõ-
ger, but that they drop into ſome
mortall finnes vpon weake temptations ; how are they like to ſtand
firme, againſt the moſt ſtrong tēp-
tations that theDiuell vfeth to propofe at the laſt houre? If in their
life, they haue byn ouercomme
by

by weake enemyes, how will they
be able to resist the most potent aduersaries? They who in their stron-
gest vnderstanding haue let fal out
of their hads the weapons of Faith,
Hope, and Charity, for want of
true art to manage them skilfully
agaynst some one temptatio; what
is like to be expected of them, whé
all the craft and force of Hell shall
assault them, that in the extremest
weakenes of body, and mind, they
shall then be able to haue a liuely
Fayth, most firme hope, and a most
perfect loue of God?

For this respect I doe most earnestly request the pious Reader,
that he be carefull to obserue this
fifth precept of the Art to dye wel,
that is, often to frequent Gods Sacraments, to accustome himselfe to
spirituall exercises, & pious works,
with this intention to arme himselfe, and to obtayne strength a-

C 5   gaynst

gaynſt that houre; and he ſhall find
by experiéce, that by this habite he
ſhall increaſe euery day in ſtrégth ,
and God will comfort him both in
the ſtormes of this life, and wil not
forſake him at the houre of death.

The ſixt Precept is , to take care to auoid
as much as may be , the committing
of veniall ſinnes , that God at our
death may be a milde Iudge vnto vs.
Chap. 8.

R EASON would require
that he that hath a ſute of great
importance before a ſeuere Iudge ,
ſhould behaue himſelfe in ſuch ſort
as he giue him no diſguſt , no not
in the ſleighteſt matter . This practice is learned from the men of
this world, who do not only ab-
ſteine warily from doing or ſaying
that which may diſpleaſe thoſe
who are to be their Iudges , and
may

may doe them harme; but on the
contrary , they ſtudy to find out
ſome meanes, that may allure them
to be propitious & fauourable vnto their cauſe, albeit herein they do
depriue themſelues of ſome commodity of good value or importance, as is dayly ſeene by the pre-
ſents of Iewels, plate, rich furniture
of all ſorts: all which albeit they be
not neceſſary if the iudge be indif-
ferent and the party haue right on
his ſide, yet for more abundant caution , they are diligent to ſeeke to
winne their fauour by ſuch means,
as are too frequently obſerued .

Now, if a man that thinketh he
hath right on his ſide, is ſo ſtudious
to make the Iudge fauorable, what
ought a Chriſtian to doe to ſecure
himſelfe before the Tribunall of ſo
ſeuere, yet moſt iuſt Iuge as Chriſt,
knowing he ſhall haue great need
of mercy? What care ſhould one
take

take to winne his fauour agaynſt
that day of ſuch infinite neceſſity?
And if by this reaſon, he who is in
doubt whether he be iuſt or no, as
for example, being not certaynely
guilty of mortall ſinne, yet piouſly
fearing leaſt he hath cōmitted ſome
is boūd to procure his Iudges fauor;
what ſhall become of him who being moſt certaine that he hath cōmitted many, & is not ſure that he
hath recouered the Iudges fauour
agayne, and moreouer knoweth
that himſelfe hath takē ſmal paines
to winne his loue? Certainely in
this caſe reaſon will conſtrayne e-
uery Chriſtian to liue with greater warines, that he doe not only
not prouoke his iudge to any new
cauſe of indignation, but that he
ſeeke by all means perfectly to pa-
cify him for the offences which in
former tymes he hath committed;
that by ſtrict reformation of his
life,

life , he may procure his fauour before he iudge him.

And for that this is the ſtate of moſt men (becauſe it is rare to find him , who hath not committed ſome , yea ſundry mortall ſinnes) therefore it is moſt proportionable for ſuch , to obſerue moſt warily this ſixth Precept , that they be not careleſſé how many veniall ſinnes they doe commit , leaſt they draw on themſelues the ſeuerity of the Iudge . Since it is neceſſary , he ſhould expect iuſtice, not mercy at the handes of the Iudge, who well knoweth the ſtuborne nature of the Criminall , that although in great matters he dare not incurre his higheſt ſeuerity, yet for ſmal offences he contemneth his fauour.

But ſome negligent Chriſtian may reply , that it is too exceſſiue rigour, to demaund of euery man to abſteyne with ſuch preciſenes to com-

commit veniall sinne, for that euery man is not obliged to frame his
life (liuing in conuersation of the
world) as if by vow he had renou-
ced the world, and had inclosed
himselfe in a Cloyster of the most
reformed Rule. But this is the common obiection of those, who seldome desire to dye well, and neuer vse to looke ouer their mortall
sins that they haue formerly committed, or know not to measure
the great danger they will be in at
their deathes. Because these who
are scarse iust, & who haue so large
a conscience that they make no
scruple to commit veniall sinnes,
runne a great hazard by their care-
lesnesse, to fall into mortall: Since
they seeme to beare small loue vnto God, and take little care to craue
his grace, without the which it is
a strage case to absteine from mortall sinne. And that soule that will
be

be so bold with his owne conscience in small faults, is most certayne to make hast vnto the brinke to fall into the pit of greater offences.

Wherfore considering this point aduisedly, I see no reason, why a Christian should be lesse circumspect, in his demeanour with God his Lord, his Creatour, his Redeemer, and his most seuere Iudge, in matters concerning his eternall saluatio nor dánation, then he would be with a mortall man, and who may be corrupted, in a matter of small moment of his remporall goods. What, are the Reformed Religious only obliged to absteine from veniall sinnes? What reason hath the secular má to assume such liberty to himselfe, so vnworthy of a pious mind, as to thinke he hath performed his duty to God sufficiently, if he haue only absteined

ned from mortall, but committeth dayly very many veniall finnes. But the deuout foule, that defireth to find Iefus a louing Father at the houre of his death, rather then a ftrict Iudge, will be more carefull then ordinary men, and will neuer think he can do inough to procure his mercy; If he remember that fearfull faying of Chrift, whē he made the world to vnderftand, that they are but few, that walke in the narrow path of life. And if there be but few that will be faued, let vs defire faluation as a moft precious & rare Iewell, and be content to take fuch extraordinary paynes and care, as mortall men do vfually take to atteyne vnto their tranfitory pleafures.

To conclude therefore, I will put the Reader in mind what Chrift fayd vnto *S. Iohn* in the laft Chapter of the Apocalyps. My tyme is
nigh

nigh; he that doth hurt, let him hurt ftill; he that is in filthines, let him be more vncleane; he that is Iuft let him yet be Iufter; and he that is Holy, let him yet be more Holy. Behold I come, and I bring my reward with me, to render to euery one according to his works. Now let the Reader take his choice: Chrift doth promife he will come fhortly, and will leaue euery man to his owne election, meaning to expreffe the fhortnes of time in this world vntil he will come to Iudge them. In the meane tyme he will haue patience with finners, permitting their malice in multiplying & heaping finnes vpon finnes, and he will giue grace vnto the Iuft to increafe in Iuftice, vntill they atteyne vnto that degree, that the wifdome of God hath ordeyned for them to receaue their reward. So that it is good counfell that

that the Iust go on in perfection of
his Iustice vntill the very houre of
his death, which he shall do, who
shall be carefull to refrayne veniall
sinnes, as vtter enemyes to his progresse in vertue.

The seauenth Precept, is to purge mãs hart
of the vanityes of this world, least
they diuert his thoughts from those
thinges, which will be necessary for
his soule, at the tyme of his death.
    Chap. 9.

HARDLY will the louers
    of this world belieue, what
great iniury they doe vnto themselues, to yield their selues cap-
tiues to the loue of the world,
neuer placing a guard vpon their
hartes. Would it might pleafe
God they could forsee, what a
fierce conflict those thinges which
they most affected, will cause them
at their death. Certainly they wold
                        much

much mortify them, which now
they paſſe ouer ſo ſleightly without remorſe of conſcience. Theſe il
aduiſed men little now conſider,
how the immoderate loue to their
childré, friends, riches, pallaces, gar-
dens, & other delights, muſt needs
proue a terrible griefe vnto their
mindes, when perforce they muſt
part with them, and they muſt be
plucked vp, from out their harts
wherein they were ſo deeply roo-
ted. Yet as if they did not know
this diſordered loue would offend
God, they plant thé dayly in their
harts, which at their dying will
proue thornes pricking their hart
with ſharpe griefe. Theſe thinges
will proue dágerous at that houre,
& when the ſoule ſhould conuert
it ſelfe cordially vñto his Lord to
finiſh well the prograſe of his life,
it will be haled ſo forcibly by theſe
inordinate affections, that the hart
will

will hardly haue power to conuert
it selfe vnto God, to craue his mercy. For the presence of those friends
who commonly vse to be about a
dying man, will leaue such an im-
pression, and cause such griefe vnto
his hart, as will alienate it from the
necessary considerations at that
tyme of heauenly & eternall ioyes.
Which is no other thing thē to hazard to forgoe his perpetuall felicity, for his corruptible goods, the
which he must leese notwithstanding.

Wherefore this seauenth precept
(to vnfasten ones hart from the
loue of transitory thinges, with intent that the soule may find herselfe
at liberty in that houre when in all
likelyhood she will be most afflicted) is full of Christian wisdome
as some few seruants of God (whō
worthily we may call spirituall
maisters) haue plainely taught vs.
For

For all their courfe of fpirituall life was nothing els, but a fequeftring their hart continually from earthly cogitations , becaufe they would not be depreffed with the weight therof, and fo leefe their high pretention to the kingdome of heaue; imitating their patterne our Sauiour, who in diuers of his actions & prayers did demonftrate a perfect feparation, euen from his moft pure mother; & according to the example of fome famous Saintes , who for our inftruction tooke extraordinary care to guarde their hartes, being vnwilling to leaue any part of their harts vnto any creature, with the leaft detriment of their inward freedome.

I thinke no man will deny, that hath any defire to dye well, that this precept is neceffary , efpecially fince I doe not require for the obferuation therof, any rare or exqui-
fite

siue affection, as that a pious man
should giue among the poore all
that is superfluous aboue his necef-
firyes, or to refraine the lawfull vse
of matrimony, both, by consent,
vowing perpetuall Chastity, the
which thinges diuers most valiant
Soldiers of Christ haue performed.
But I demaund no such hard matter, but only, that who loueth his
owne safety would haue a care not
to let his hart be too fast tyed vnto
the pleasures of this earth. And this
caution is proportionable to all
states and conditions, and heerein
no man can excuse himselfe, with
saying he is marryed, he must attêd
his temporall estate. I say none can
excuse themselues, because this coû-
sel doth not forbid a sufficient loue
or orderly affection according to
the lawful obligatiô of euery mans
calling: but only serueth to moderate excessiue affection, such as will

6

pre-

preiudice the liberty of the soule.
For *Iob* was marryed, and among
other diligences which he tooke,
one was, not to fixe his hart too
much on any thing, saying: *If I*
haue reioyced in my great wealth, and
becaufe my hand found many riches. Iob.
31. as if he would haue faid: Good
Lord, thou knowest that I neuer
setled my affection vpō my riches,
nor thofe many temporall pleafurs
that I had in my poffeffion .

The fame moderate affection
he bare vnto his Children, as may
well appeare by his pious gouer-
ninge them, offering vp Sacrifice
for them, that they might not fixe
their hartes too ferioufly on the
goods, and delightes of the earth.
Dauid likewife was married, and he
gaue vnto others this wife Coūfell
wch he pr____ed himfelfe: *If ri-*
ches doe abound, fe: __i you____ __
them. Pfal. 61. He fayeth not, Doe
not

not poffeife riches , but doe not
fuffer your hart to delight in them.
Thefe wordes proceeded from a
wife man , who knew well , that
the riches of this world doe vfe to
draw the hart of a man vnto them
very forcibly. Queene *Hefter* was
married to fo great an eftate of riches and worldly glory, as was
thought fhe could enioy no greater on earth, yet fhee liued with
that circumfpection , and warines
leaft her hart might adhere vnto
thofe riches which the vaine world
adored, that in time of her prayers
with earneft affectiõ fhe vfed thefe
wordes vnto God as follow : *Lord*
thou knoweft my mind that I do abhorre
the figne of my pride & glory that ador-
neth my head , when I fhew my felfe a-
broad ; and I deteft the fame in the dayes
of my filence, as the   of a   ; in
*   s. Heft. 14 . Which*
wordes do intimate a mind that
did

did keepe watch with great care,
that the idle alluringe vanities of
this life should not enthrall her
hart, and curbe the liberty of the
spirit, which shee esteemed aboue
all the kingdomes in the world.

Well then, if such great Princes
in the midest of such occasiōs could
liue with this freedome of their
harts, it will follow that ordinary
men in lesse occasions may easily
obserue this precept. The which
we may see , euen in these our
dayes, that among so many that
haue little feare of God, there is
found some few not only Religious, but also secular, that in the midest of the busines of the world do
set this Centinell on their hart ,
& do euery day expect their death,
and thirst after the eternall riches
of heauen. And if these whome I
haue named had such care not too
much to set their affection on their
D moor

moueable riches, & their Honour:
what extraordinary diligence is to
be vfed in thofe things, wnich haue
more force to attract our hart vnto
them, I meane our naturall childré,
efpecially our heyres ? For there
mufi needs be great odds between
the naturall loue to our children,
& our temporall goods. Wherefore
I recommend vnto the Reader a
mofi wary cufiody of his hart from
the doting loue of his children and
fome of his deerefi friends, & other
fuch like affections , & that he may
doe it the better, he had need to in-
uocate the mercy and grace of our
Sauiour to affifi him .

The

The eight Precept , is not to engage him-
selfe into too many businesse, least they
distract his mind at his death for that
they are not finished. Chap. 10.

THOSE who are trauelling
home into their Countrey,&
haue their only desire to come safe
after a long iourney, do not vse to
entangle themselues with intricate
businesse in those places which in
hast they are to passe through , and
if by necessity any businesse do occurre that may hinder them, they
labour by all the meanes they can
to dispatch the same, that they may
cōtinue their iourney homewards.
This is a most certayne verity, and
consented vnto by all, and so conformable to common sense, that it
cannot rest in the mind of any pru-
dent man to vndertake new businesse, where there is no likelihood
D 2   that

that eyther he may finith them , or be in any hope to enioy the pleasant fruite of his toylesome labour. And if a passenger fortune to be delighted with some one more pleasant place then other , and he findeth a disposition to enter into his hart to remayne & trafique in that place , reason presently telleth him that , that negotiation will much crosse his first important necessityes, and that it were a foolish thing to make long aboad in a strange place , since he must of necessity returne to his natiue Countrey.

A Christian therefore, making profession that in all the variety of wayes in this world, he is to passe but as a Pilgrime , and alwayes aime at the most pleasant Citty of God Heauenly *Ierusalem,* the common Countrey of the elect, eyther he ought to abstaine to engage him-

himselfe into affayres which he will neuer see perfectly finished in his life, or els he must confesse, that his thoughts are not principally directed vnto that Coūtrey, wherin he desireth euer to rest : For it is too grosse an errour to go about to perswade any man be he neuer so simple , much lesse to deceaue God who searcheth the secrets of mans hart , that he who willingly puzzelleth his thoughts with many troublesome busines of this world , can freely eleuate his hart to heauen. From hence we may discerne the obscurity and grosse blindnes of many , not only marryed-men but also the Clergy, that with great guilt of their conscience (for resisting Gods often inspirations that admonish them to set an end vnto the multiplicity of their negotiations , and to thinke of their soules, and prepare themselues for their

D 3   death)

death) will neuer cut off their bu-
finesse, vntill Gods iustice cut off
their liues, with great vnquietnes
of their côscience, who dye in that
confused manner. And if they will
examine the originall cause of this
great mischiefe, they shall find it
was, becaufe at firft they gaue thé-
felues too much liberty to enter into fo many affayres one after another, neuer finishing fo much as
one: and permitted their fenfes to
be captiuated with auarice, tranfported with ambitiõ, incited with
anger, and misfled with other paf-
fions, which would not fuffer thé
ftedily to prepare for their ineuitable death. I know not how thefe
trauailers are blinded, that they cãnot fee thefe fnares that are pitched
in their way, but they willingly
bind their feet in them, that they
cannot walke on, & keep the fore-
right-way of Chriftian piety, and
the

the path that leadeth to eternall
life .

Now let vs suppose that some
malignant feuer do surprize those
that are thus confounded with multitude of businesse , into which
their owne variety of affections
haue lead them captiue , and none
of them as yet brought to any perfectiō : How can a man in this sort
distempered with so pestilent a feuer, (as he hardly can with true attētion call vpon the name of God)
quietly and securely giue commis-
sion to any other, and rest confident that they wil be wel finished ?
His affayres will require a sound
brayne, & a quiet iudgement, long
tyme, & great industry , so to dispose all thinges in the feare of God,
without iniustice to any , or iniury to his neighbour. How then cā
this be , since he is hardly in his
senses? He cannot apply his mind,

D 4   he

he wanteth tyme , for he is in all
haſt called vnto the iudgement of
God .

Theſe are no fictions, nor yet
fall out ſo ſeldome as they are not
probably to be expected; but ſo ordinary , and haue giuen ſo horride
examples, as might wel mooue the
moſt ſtony and obdurate hart vnto compunction . Whereupon ſome
few that feare God, who haue many buſineſſe, and yet in the mideſt
of their buſineſſe haue a deſire to
dye well, who peraduenture heer-
tofore haue been to blame in this
point; when they call to mind that
eyther by their age, or their weakenes, their tyme of death is like to
approach , they rayſe their ſpirits
with great force , they burſt the
nettings wherin they were ſtrayte
tyed; nay albeit with great detriment of their temporall fortunes ,
they caſt from them all impedi-
                              ments,

ments, they retyre themselues from all worldly distractions, least they should haue the least occasion of perturbation at the houre of death, when they ought to attend with all their hart to conclude the bargayne of their eternall saluation. And our barren age hath not failed to produce some few wise-men of this sort, who haue deliuered ouer their Kingdomes, with all their worldly busines, vnto their heires and retyred themselues with most rare example of piety, to prepare only to entertayne most willingly their dayly expected death.

Now let the Reader well aduise with himselfe, whether he will be one of those who haue such multiplicity of businesse, that hauing no end, may so violently assault him at the houre of his death, or els be free from all worldly affections, to be ready to meete with his Lord

D 5 when

when he shall demaund an accopt
of his life, and must receyue at his
hands eyther eternall ioy, or euerlasting payne.

The ninth precept, is to exercise those acts
of vertue as are most necessary for the
houre of death.   Chap. 11.

IF I now had that vnderstadin-
ge of the loue of God, and charity towards my neighbor that some
haue who are more illumined by
God, I should feele great compassion, & in this place might earnestly bewayle the carelesse negligéce,
and inconsideration of Christians.
That whereas they vse to forecast,
and warily consider, vnto a word,
what speach is necessary that they
vse vnto a man like vnto theselues,
fearinge to take some disgrace by
comittinge some small errour: yet
they scare not the iustice of God,
                              nor

nor take any care to prepare, or to
study those actes of vertue that are
fittest to stand them insteed at their
passage out of this world, to performe their duty vnto God, and a-
gainst those cruell enemyes who
will most fiercely assault them in
their greatest weaknes. And to me
it seemeth most strange that a man
may meet with diuers graue men,
who in their moral discourses may
seeme fit to gouerne a kingdome
with their worldly wisedome; but
if one should exhort them to performe some noble act of faith, as to
resolue to suffer martyrdome of
some Infidel or Tyrant that should
compell them to renounce their
Christian faith; or an act of Hope,
as if they should seeme to be at the
very gates of hell, yet then to rely
most confidently on our Sauiours
passion; or an act of true Contri-
tio, as if they were by some necessi-
D 6   ty

ty to dye, without the aide of some good Confessour to giue them the Sacraments, and helpe to instruct them ; therin you shall finde them mute and not able to expresse any forme of true loue of God ; or demonstrate such intensiue sorrow for hauing grieuously offended so louing a God, as that they who are about them, may haue any consolation from them .

Oh what meaneth this blinde ignorance! What may one thinke of this their alienation from God. What, doth all greatnes and wisedome consist in tumbling downe Cittyes, and ruinating of kingdomes? or doth it not rather consist in possessinge a Noble hart, that can despise this vaine world? Or to be able to help himselfe with actes of piety, & to resist death, & preuaile against the fury of hell, at that time when worldly wit, strength, and

sub-

subtilty muſt faile all men? What good is it for a great Lord of the Earth to cut off the heads of many Princes, if he doe not know, ncr deſire to learne how to manage his ſpirituàll weapons, with which is wonne the kingdome of heauen? Oh, what a profitable matter wold it be, if Chriſtiãs would arme them ſelues in time, and exerciſe thoſe actes of vertue, which at their laſt houre may comfort them, & open for them the gate of heauen . Certainely it is not likely, that at that hower (wherin there are ſo many obiects of feare & motiues of amazement, the ſpirits ſo feeble, the repreſentation of our foule ſinnes paſt ſo terrible, the terrour of preſent death, and horrour of our iudgement following, Hell gates ſet wide open for vs) a man ſhall haue power to make an act of firme cōfidence in God , who in his life hath

hath not practifed, or fo coldly, or weakly exercifed thofe acts, as was to fmal purpofe to obtain the habit of fuch vertues, as one fhall haue great need of in his laft paflage.

Therefore he that will proceed wifely, let him exercife the acts of Fayth, Hope, and Charity often in his beft helth, efteeminge them as precious treafures, and delicious fruits of the paffiõ of Iefus Chrift, which muft helpe him to get the victory of the world, the flefh, and the Diuell. And if a man haue any defire to dye well, he fhall finde this Counfell (to exercife thefe actes vpon many occafions in ones helth) to be of infinite importance againft many accidents of loffe of fenfe, or fpeach, or fudden death. For it may be that thefe former actes may faue his foule when he can not make fruitfull vfe of the Sacraments, and without eyther

of

of thefe meanes it is moſt difficult
to be faued . And becaufe it is the
higheſt point of wifedome as the
Deuines hold to make thefe three
actes of the Theologicall Vertues
purely and perfectly, it will not be
amiſſe to prefent vnto the Reader
a certaine Memoriall , the which
many great feruants of God haue
highly eſteemed. This is, to referue
if it were but one quarter of an
houre euery day to retire thefelues
into fome Oratory or priuate place, and imagininge themfelues to
be a dying , and to be tempted eyther with infidelity , or diffidence
in fome hygh point of faith, or hatred againſt the feuerity of Gods
Iuſtice , or with delight in fome
finne .

From thefe temptatiõs it is eafy
to frame fome actes of Fayth, Hope
and Charity, which may proue a
moſt profitable and ready meanes

to

to dye well . For by vsinge these
actes in health, which are of necessity in sicknes, in the houre of death
they will be familiar vnto them,
and will bringe with them great
consolation to their soules if they
haue any vnderstanding left . And
if they fall senseles, yet shall they
reape the reward of those actes,
which they practised when they
were in their perfect vnderstan-
dinge . This aduantage other negligent men shall want, as is to
often apparent to such as attend
them at their death.

The tenth precep:, is to resist couragious-
ly temptations, least the saule at the
houre of death be ouercome therwith.
Chap . 12.

IT can not be expressed in wordes, of what importance this
Counsell (to resist, and cut off the
heades

heades of temptations at their firſt
ſuggeſtions) will be vnto vs , at
that time when the Diuell doth
enforce himſelfe to doe his worſt.
Knowinge that if then he faile of
the victory, the prey he ſo much
coueteth will ſlyp immediatly out
of his fingers . And I need not labour to explicate , what all good
Chriſtians doe belieue ; That the
conflict of that houre being moſt
ſharpe, a man had need of the more
courage & ſtrength to defend himſelfe . And if it be agreed on , that
there wil be great need of actiuity,
and conſtancy at that houre, it wil
conſequently follow , there ought
to be fit preparation before . This
preparation is one of the principall
points of the doctrine of the Croſſe of Chriſt, becauſe it is moſt op-
poſite vnto the appetites of our
Carnality . And it vſeth to produce moſt admirable effects in ſuch,
	as

as painefully practice this science.
For besides the ordinary mortification that it causeth of our brutish
appetites, and the great profit of
meriting present grace and future
glory; it breedeth in a man a noble
and generous courage, scorning to
render him selfe captiue. It is an
armour of proofe to keepe him
from being wounded by the fierce
blowes of his enraged enemy.

To which purpose it wil be necessary to ponder the meaning of
Holy Church the spouse of Christ,
who by the Counsell of the diuine
wisedôme, euery day repeateth the
wordes of *S. Peter: Breethren be yee
sober, and keep watch, for that your Aduersary the Diuell, like a roaring Lion
runneth round about, spyinge whome he
may denoure, whome yee must resist stron-
ge in faith.* This watch needs not
dayly be set, if there were not euident daunger. This Coate-armour
                    should

should not euery day be put on , if
the neceffity were not eminent, or
vnleife it were very likely that this
rauenous beaft would euery day
affault vs. For we fee by experience that yonge Children and old
men dye indifferently euery day.
This being true, we muft needes
aproue the meaning of the Church
to be, to intimate to all without
diftinction , by dayly repeatinge
this faying , that euery day we
should prepare for our laft battell:
exercifinge our ftrength with the
fortitude of Fayth to refifte , and
aduifing vs that our onely armour
of proofe will be a ftoute courage
neuer to giue foote backe from the
enemy . Oh, that all Chriftians
might receyue fuch cleare light
from the bouty of God , to difcerne
the conueniency of this celeftiall
doctrine , but efpecially Church-
men , whofe obligation is dayly

to reade it, & whofe infinite comfort will be perpetually to follow it. And ponder well the fore fayd wordes of the Apoftle, which expreffe a great Chriftian zeale of the militant Church, which dayly muft combat with her vifible, and inuifible perfecutours.

But it is greatly to be lamēted, that there are very few who reading thefe words, and being placed as Centinells for others fafety, they doe not make fo good vfe of the words for their owne felues as they fhould; but they will one day repent it I feare, when it wil be too late. For the truth is, that the crafty Diuell obferuing thefe to ftep backe, and to fall, and to be faint-harted-cowardes, commeth vpon them with greater prefumption, feing the fault to proceed from thēfelues, & perceauing they come into the field vnarmed, he fuppo-
                                    feth

seth they are abandoned from the Campe of Christ, he presently mustereth vp all his internall legions, vsing vnto them the wordes of the Psalme: *God hath forsaken him. follow him, for there is no body to deliuer him out of my handes . Psal. 70.* This boldnes the Diuell assumeth , when he obserueth the base mind, or euill correspondence, or small cooperatiō of any man with the grace of God. But on the contrary when he findeth a soule resolute, prompt, faythfull, armed with Gods grace, who still smites of the head , or dasheth out the braynes of euery little temptation , vpon the rocke of fayth, the Rascall slinkes away, enuying to giue a man any occasion of new victories. And the soule goeth on couragiously , increaseth in strength, and with admirable vigour performeth her last combat at the houre of death: and parting

L

ting out of this world fighting,
scornefully derideth the Diuell, &
immediatly at Gods handes receyueth an Eternall crowne of glory.

The eleauenth Precept, is to appropriaté
   some little tyme to consider the Agony
   of Death, doing some acts of Vertue,
   to obtayne patience, and conformity
   with Chrißts paßion. Chap. 13.

THE consideration and premeditation of future euills,
doth ease or diminish the disgust
therof, and in deuout soules it produceth a great effect of piety, as
may be proued by those, who with
the spirit and desire to be saued doe
spend sometime in considering the
last most sower relish of death. The
reason of this doctrine is apparent.
For, a Christian to setle himselfe to
consider the Agony of Death, and
represent vnto his senses the an-
                              guish

guish and perills that accompany
his death , is no other thing then a
manner of often dying, and confe-
quently to make it more familiar
with him, and to fweeten the bitternes thereof, by the operation of
Gods grace: in fuch fort that when
true death doth come in earneft , it
finds the foule prepared with long
expectation of it, & it feemeth nothing fo ftrange,and terrible as if it
had come vnlooked for. But that
which helpeth moft men is , that
the often refoluing to endure that
Agony patiently , in conforming
our felues with Chrift his dying
for vs , caufeth at our death our
foule to find it felfe disburdened of
feare, and armed agaynft the de-
ceites of the Diuell . There is no
doubt but this forethinking of our
death, worketh much good againft
that houre, and at the prefent caufeth a forcible reformation of a mãs
                              life,

life, and correcteth his vices: **But**
all the difficulty confisteth in fpa-
ring a little tyme for this confideration . But he that hath a defire to
paffe that agony , without woun-
ding of his foule, wil neuer efteeme
it tedious, to affigne certainly one
halfe an houre , or a quarter euery
day, deliberatly to confider his laft
battayle . For with this fo moderate a labour, reducing into his
memory his final end, he fhal make
a competent preparation for his
death .

For out of this confideration do
arife many fruits of vertue , which
will produce great increafe at all
tymes, but wil infinitely multiply
themfelues at the laft houre: wheras diuers fcandalls doe arife from
many , yea Religious Profeffours ,
who hauing neglected to accu-
ftome themfelues with that ma-
ture deliberation , as the weight of
that

that cause iuftly requireth, when
they muft be told they can not efcape, on a fuddaine they feeme fo
to be confounded, that they afforde
very poore edification vnto fuch as
attēd them. And befides the harme
of ill example they leaue vnto o-
thers, they are the caufe of intollerable mifchiefe vnto themfelues.
For the vnwelcome tydinges that
they can liue no longer, doth affright their hart in fuch fort, that all
freedome is takē from them to put
their foule in order, and with true
feruor of fpirit to call vpon God, or
fruitfully to vfe his Sacraments as
they are obliged. But their hart only laboureth to feeke after cure of
their body, impioufly neglecting
the eternall life of both foule and
body.

And that which is worft of all,
if any do Counfell them to attend
to their foule, they expreffe fuch a
E   deale

deale of impatience & willfull re-
pugnancy to the pleafure of God,
that it maketh euery one loath to
aduife them, for feare of augmen-
ting their vnquietnes. And by this
meanes, fome dye without makinge of their wils, fome without
their finall viaticum, fome without
confeffion. And befides thefe fpirituall loffes, fome dye rauinge, fome
fpeechles, fome confeffe they are
vifibly tormented in this world
by the Diuell; that it is apparent
that the Iuftice of God beginneth
to giue them in this life a triall of
their future condition rather for o-
thers admonition, thē their proper
good, fince they were fo careles to
obtaine his mercy, when they
might haue procured it.

Oh, how many manifeft fignes
of reprobation do appeare in many
fuch perfons in their very paffage,
that before in health would not
render

render themselues voluntarily vnto the sweet pleasure of God, but by
all meanes fastened their affections
to this teporall life, vntill the arme
of Iustice was extended on them,
& they deliuered ouer as a prey
vnto death and hell. At last arri-
ueth the houre wherin the iust sentence is executed vpon the vniust
man, and he is violently haled from
his life he doted on; and it may
seeme God vttereth these wordes
against him with a terrible sound:
Let his confidence be pulled out of
his Tabernacle, and let destruction
trample on him like a Tirant . But
from these woes are they deliuered,
who wisely with an humble spirit
premeditate what will succeede .
For this reason it is good Counsell to consult with ones selfe, con-
cerninge this busines of so much
weight; at some conuenient time
appointed for that purpose, as those

refor-

reformed Religious vfe to doe, that among the meditations that are deuided for the dayes of the week, one of them is appointed for that fubiect of their fpirituall profit.

Now, I would wifh the reader to lay afide the idle opinion of the world, & not to giue credit to carnall friendes, who may perhaps thinke, that the obferuation of this precept may fill the minde with Melancoly, & as it were bury him quick before his time. But it is nothing fo. For pious peniter thoghts (although they may produce teares of Contrition) are of another nature. They do not make one melancolike fadd, but do comfort by eleuating the foule. For true contrition purgeth the foule frõ finne, which did depreffe it: and althogh carnal cogitations apprehed it will caufe heauines, yet in fpirituall mindes it is ful of ineftimable con-
                            fola-

folation. Becaufe it begetteth a
moft liuely and confident hope,
replenifhed with all cordiall ioy.
Since all operations of Gods Iuftice are comfortable, according to
verfe of the Pfalme : *The Iuftices of
God are right, makinge the hart ioyfull;
the precept of God is cleare, illuminating
mens eyes. Pfal. 18.* But let vs graunt,
that the premeditation of death did
make one fadd, in fuch fort as the
louers of the world apprehend, it
were good Counfell notwithftanding to purchafe eternall ioy with
temporall fadnes, according vnto
the faying of the Gofpell : Bleffed
are they who fhall mourne, for
they fhall be recomforted.

*The twelfth precept is, euery morninge to
refolue fo to fped that day, as if it were
to be the laft of our life.* Chap. 14.

THIS Counfell is found to
be of that efficacy, as thofe
E 3 few

few spirituall persons that are liuing, & would imitate the ancient Saints, doe labour to obserue the same with much more strictnes, then I doe require. Because they finde by experience it is a great furtherance to liue with greater perfection, and to finde themselues ready when death shall assault thẽ. I say with greater strictnes, because they are not only contented to renew this purpose once or twice a-day, but in euery action they begin, they apply this intention: as if euery action were to be their vttermost, and as if at the end therof, they should be sommoned to the Iudgement of God.

For who is he that cannot discerne how it must needes follow, that if a man doe so guide himselfe euery day, as if he were that euening to appeare before the Iudgement of God; it must needes conse-

se-

fequently make him ready both
in ftate of foule, and patience of
minde; although his death come
not in many yeares after. Let but
the reader confider with him felfe,
that if it were reuealed vnto him,
that this very day he fhould dye,
with what affection would he doe
all his actions? There is no doubt
but he would doe all thinges with
more fincerity, then otherwife he
would. Now will it follow, that
he who fo doth without reuelatiõ,
muft needes be better prepared, if
by chance it fhould fo fall out,
which prudently he prouided for
before.

This doctrine hath wrought
great good in the reformed Con-
uents of Religious people. Which
if the dull world do not as yet obferue, yet future times muft needes
make all men to acknowledge. But
fome may mocke, and aske to what

E 4   pur-

purpose should I euery day do a-
new that which I finde certainely
to be otherwise then I haue so
longe expected? This is nothing
els then to hold that for certaine
euery morninge, which the next
eueninge will proue false. Such a
wiseman I desire to pay in his own
money, demaunding of him be he
neuer so worldly; For what end
doth he lay his snares euery day to
get transitory riches, since he is not
sure euery day to increase the same?
To what end doth he attend the
Princes court euery day, for some
temporall or spirituall preferment,
since he is certayne that euery day
he shall not, nor cannot obtaine
new promotions? But he will answer; It is true I can not gaine them
euery day, but I may haue them v-
pon some one day, & because that
day to me is so vncertaine, therefore it behooueth me to leese no
one

one day in seeking for them . Oh
worldly man , canst thou be so diligent for thy body , and so negligent for thy soule? Yet this answer
doth confesse the conueniency of
this precept . For if the louers of
the world (grounding their imagination on a doubtfull accident,
as in the procuring of some Ec-
clesiasticall or Temporall dignity)
doe not omit to doe their best seruice, as if they were to gaine it e-
uery day : why should not a Christian much more doe his ordinary
workes , as he would do them , if
he did know that should be his last
day, it being most certaine that one
of the (& he knoweth not which)
must be his last?

The vaine louers of this present life will not practice this verity : but their errour ought to be a
greater incitement to those who
loue God to argue thus with them-

felues. The common errour of fuch as treade the large path is, to defire to liue euer in this world if they could, & the fecureft wifedome of thofe few iuft who keep the narrow path, is to efteeme themfelues as already condemned to dye, looking euery day for their execution. Therefore it is fafer to adhere to this fecond fenfe, and fo to liue euery day, as if for certainely it were to be the laft. Thus liued the Primitiue Martyrs, expectinge each day, that the Tyrants would put them to death. And the Confeffours of fingular Sanctity did euery day pronounce vnto themfelues their one deaths, watching euery houre for it, and animating themfelues to worke with moft cordiall affections, as if the next day after they fhould haue no more time to merit in, & to negotiate their faluation.

And

And certainely it is the voyce of a Iuſt man to pronounce theſe wordes of the Apoſtle: *I dye euery day.* 1. *Cor.* 15. And with theſe I will finiſh this Chapter, exhorting euery one to imprint this ſentence in his ſoule, in ſuch ſort as he may expreſſe it in his actions. And as the Apoſtle did euery day make oblation of himſelfe, to be willing to dye (for that is the meaninge of thoſe wordes;) ſo the pious man who hath a deſire to end the courſe of his life happily, wil expoſe himſelfe euery day to death, with the like affection as had thoſe Martyrs, when really they exchanged their preſent Pilgrimage for their eternall country.

E 6 *The*

*The thirteenth precept is , to examine
euery day his Confcience , as if prefently he were to render vp his laft
account .   Chap. 15.*

I Doe fuppofe that a Chriftian
doth not feare Death, becaufe it
taketh him out of this world , but
in refpect of the Iudgment of God
which immediatly followeth death. Therefore euery mans preparation muft aime at this point efpecially . He therefore is well prepared that hath wel ordered his ac-
counts of all his actions. And therfore the Euangelift S. *Matthew* recounteth , that as foone as Iefus-
Chrift had fayed thefe wordes ;
*Watch , for that yee do not know the day
nor houre.* Cap. 15. then immediatly
followeth the Parable of the Mai-
fter that would make a iourney into a tarre Countrey, and called his
                                       fer-

feruants, and diftributed talents to
euery one, and then he fayth : After
a while the Mayfter called thofe
feruants to make their accompt ,
which is as much as to fay , When
Chrift calleth men vnto him by
the fommons of their death, he thē
calleth them to an accompt of the
Talents that he imparted vnto thē.
Now, who knoweth not the ftrict
accoūt that the ftewards of Princes
& other inferiour officers haue that
are to giue vp their accompts of all
vnder their charge? It were not eafy
to conceiue the ftrictnes thereof, if
it were not dearely bought by cō-
mon experience.

If this be fo, what wifer coun-
fel can be prefcribed vnto him that
is to render an accompt vnto a Seuere Lord, then diligently to keep
a Regifter, wherein he may dayly
write downe what he layeth out
or receyueth, leaft on a fodayne he
be

be called, and his reckoning not set downe distinctly he may be much confouded before his Lord. A man can hardly expresse what diligece some good men vse in this point, who besides al other recordations, do keep so punctuall a note of the smal sinns they commit euery day, least they should forget to confesse them on the greatest sodain occasion. And not fully satisfyed with this dayes note, they doe reduce vnto certayne heades, the whole tyme of their life, with so curious obseruation of numbers, tymes, & places, that although some sodaine accident may befall them, they wil be able on a sodaine to make a perfect general confession of each part of their life, without any corporall toyle, or perturbation of minde, expressing true affection of contrition, and receyuing (in the midest of their sorrow) abundant profit,

by

by their pious & laudable preuention of tyme .

This is the diligence and prudence of good men, that in a matter of such moment as is their eternall saluation, they are not contented with small industry , but they
incline and strayne vnto the more
secure, more holy, and more comfortable, and yet most easy way in
their life, & at their death the most
profitable . And besides this , for
further satisfaction of their owne
conscience , they vse so fayhtfull a
methode of sifting their conscience , that besides the ordinary dayly examination thereof, which
all reformed Religious orders doe
make , they doe hourely not only
examine their actions one by one ,
but they vse to pronounce a most
terrible sentence of Gods iustice a-
gainst themselues , as the vpright
ministers of Gods true Iustice . In
      such

such sort, that as often as they commit the smallest offence, they instantly impose vpon themselues some such pennance, as a discreet confessour would enioyne his penitent for the like trespasse. These be the faythfull workemen, that will not be burdened at the houre of their death, because in them will be verifyed those wordes of the Apostle : *If we would truly iudge our selues, we should not be iudged by God*. The Grandies, the Rich, the Proud, & subtile men of the world will not take this so tedious a toyle (for so it appeareth to them) strictly to iudge their owne actions, but wil heap vp fuell for God to set on fire in Hell in the day of his most seuere Iudgement. But let them doe as they list, I wish the Reader who feareth God, to imitate the exáple of the Iust, if he will confidently appeare in the presence of God.

The

*The fourteenth Precept , is to vse some
kind of mortification voluntary vpon
our body, that the paynes of death may
not seeme so terrible, as the Soule may
keese the sense of God.* Chap. 16.

TO mortify the body is nothing els , but in conuenient
tyme , and by degrees , to learne it
to beare death with more patience.
For we find by experience , that
when the body is afflicted with a
long and tedious sicknes, the soule
is more willing to leaue it, as a noi-
some prison, and doth dayly expect death as a day of liberty, as we
read in diuers Epistles of S. *Gregory*
the Great, who was exercised by
God with many sharpe infirmi-
tyes, and grieuous torments . Ad-
mitting this which is manifest, he
that is tryed by God with such vi-
sitations, which cause this present
life

life to seeme tedious, if one would
season them and sanctify them, he
must himselfe practise some mortifications, which may so disquiet his
body as may take away or destroy
the quicke carnality, which causeth
it to be so sensible of euery sleight
payne. For certainly, if you let it
still enioy its ease, it will so delight
in cherishing & pampering it selfe,
that at his death euery ordinary
payne will trouble it exceedingly,
and diuert it from attending vnto
any thing that shall appertaine vnto God.

They who fat the body, & nice-
ly cherish it, ought to consider, that
such delicacies do bind the soule in
that pot of earth, and causeth it to
take so deep roote, that there will
be need of very great force to pull
it vp agayne. And therefore it will
be the wiser way, to loosen the
roote by little & little, that it may
more

more eafily yield; and fo to beguile
it with a holy deceit, that we may
dye by degrees, whiles we liue, as
diuers holy Saintes haue giuen vs
example, who by fafting and other
rigours haue approached to one degree of death in their beft health,
that there apeared nothing on thē
but bones couered with a dry skin,
as is reported of holy *Saint Bafill* the
great . Thofe true fpirituall men
who obferue this precept of mortifying their bodyes, feeme iuft to do
as wife Merchants, who traueling
on the fea in a great ftorme, are cō-
pelled oftentymes for the laft re-
fuge to faue their liues, to disburdē
the fhip, cafting ouer boord many
wares of good value, which they
hartly loued.

There is no queftion, but that e-
uery one loueth his owne flefh
withall his hart, but we muft imagine we are in the fwelling waues
                                    of

of the troubled Sea of this world, through the which very few vessels passe secure without danger of shipwracke : and he that will haue his owne be one of those few that passe safe, must disburden his ship of those thinges he most estemeth, that his soule may be secured. So did the Apostle, who albeit he had the first fruits of the Spirit, by vertue whereof it was probable he might haue strongly borne vp any weight of his body, yet he exercised himselfe in mortifying of his body ; *for feare* (as his owne words are) *least he might become a reprobate*. This Apostolicall doctrine haue the iust learned, and imitated valiantly agaynst their owne flesh and punishing their owne bodyes, for to gaine spirituall strength, & with a certayne agility to passe through the narrow gate of heauen.

But some will say, that these
                                    thinges

thinges were rare , rather to be admired then imitated , and not to be
performed by euery one . I muſt
anſwere them that will ſay thus, as
S. *Auguſtine* replyed vnto ſuch an
obiection , which he made vnto
himſelfe in this manner : Some
may aske , who is he that can tread
the ſteps of the Martyrs ? We may
imitate (S. *Auguſtine* ſayth) not only the actions of the Martyrs , but
alſo of Chriſt himſelfe , by the aſſi-
ſtance of his grace. The which may
be proued by reaſon . For leauing
apart all other vertues, & to ſpeake
only of this mortifying of the fleſh,
we may obſerue the body of our
bleſſed Sauiour in the agony of his
bitter paſſion, more tormented and
torne, then the mortifications of S.
Paul , or S. *Baſill* could euer come
nigh . But ſuppoſe that he ſuffered
to the end that we ſhould imitate
him in what we are able , yet I
would

would not haue the Reader fticke
faft in this difficulty , but paffe it o-
uer, becaufe my mind is not to perfwade any mã to vfe fuch rare mortifications , but rather to haue a pious defire , and vfe moderate practice to difcharge his foule from the
oppreffion of the flefh, leaft the fpirit be fo much borne downe by the
weight of the flefh , that it indure
more payne and gayne leffe merit,
& call on the Mercyes of God with
fmall zeale, and affection at the
houre of death .

The fifteenth Precept, conteineth certaine
    particuler diligences to moone our
    Sauiour the fooner to giue vs his gra-
    ce to dye well.   Chap. 17.

I Will reduce thefe diligences
  which in my opinion are moft
neceffary for this art of dying well
vnto three heades . The firft fhall
                                    be

be concerning the workes of Charity. The second of the Sacrifice of the Altar. The third perteyning to feruent perfeuerance in prayer. As concerning the firft, I doe fuppofe that death is the laft of the miferies of mans life, and that he who is in finne vnpurged, will find himfelfe in fo miferable a cafe at his paffage, that it it were to be fenfibly decerned by vs that do liue, certainly it would côuert the moft ftony hart into tender côpaffion. The which we are bound to belieue by thofe wordes which the Church, the Spoufe of Chrift, doth commonly vfe, when we are to vifit and affift thofe who are nigh their deaths, expreffing therby the extreme need they are in.

Now then, if a Chriftian do vnderftand that he fhall find himfelfe inftantly in moft extreme pouerty and mifery, what wifer or fitter

Coun-

Counsell can he take hold on, the
firſt prouiding for his owne neceſ-
ſityes, do as many workes of Charity as he may, helping ſuch as God
hath layd at our mercy, that they
praying for vs to relieue their wāts,
their prayers may obtayne mercy
for vs in our extreme neceſſity at
the houre of death. The promiſe of
our Lord Ieſus is vniuerſall: *Bleſſed
are the mercifull, for that they ſhall obteyne mercy. Matth.* 5. The which S.
Luke confirmeth in theſe wordes:
*I ſay vnto you, Make friendes vnto your
ſelues of the Mammon of iniquity, that at
what tyme yee ſhall fayle, they may receaue you into the euerlaſting Taber-
nacles, Luc.* 16. And *S. Laurence* at
his death vpon the hoat Gridyron
anſwered the Emperour demāding
where were the Riches which he
was told the Chriſtian Prieſts had
when they offered vp the Sacrifice
of the Maſſe in Chalices of gold:
                                    The

The handes (sayd he) of the poore haue layed them vp safe among the Heauenly Treasures.

Now the if Chrifts promife be to all, no doubt it is fitting for the diuine verity to teftify this corefpondence in fuch a tyme; in which he that hath performed what Christ appointed him, is in the greateft neceffity, of that which Christ promifed him. And agayne, if he who did that mercyfull deed, did it with that intention to find mercy at the houre of his death, Chrift in Iuftice will not defraude him of the reward he annexed to the deed: and therefore due likewife vnto his attention, who feemed fo to haue concluded the bargaine. Therefore for this reafon let euery man when he doth giue Almes to the poore, or comfort the diftreffed, harbour poore pilgrimes, or any other worke of mercy, let him

F   I

I say, call this point to memory, and doe the same with that particuler intention, to find mercy at Gods handes in his greatest desolation at the houre of his death.

The second is of greater importance, as those few doe best find who haue worthily esteemed of the value and efficacy of this most holy and Diuine Sacrament of the body and bloud of the new Testament of Iesus Christ: The greatest miracle of all Miracles, and most perfect pledge left with vs to testify his loue. That which euery one is to doe concerning this point is, if he be a Priest, to say his Masses with this one intention among some others, to obtayne at his death to be in the fauour of God. If he be a Lay-man, when he procureth any Masses to be said to his intention, let this intention alwayes be one, putting an assured

sured confidence in the vertue of
this powerfull and faythfull Sacrifice , and belieuing that in all
his life, and with all his inuention
he cannot vse a more profitable
diligence, then this to obtayne a
good death . In this place I cannot let passe, to put some ill Christians in remébrance of their great
improuidence , or rather of their
abiect and base conceyte in this
point, who being more Carnall
then Spirituall , when they find
themselues in any temporall perplexity, will make recourse vnto
this mysticall Sacrifice , by procuring Masses to be offered eyther to
come well out of, or end such a
businesse , or suite in Law, or to
obtayne some thing they pretend
concerning this world ; but few
there be that vse the same diligence to pray for a quiet & happy
death .

F 2   The

The third Point, is often prayer & feruent petition at Gods hands for a good death, esteeming that as the most singular and most necessary benefit that one may receaue of him. But this petition is not to be made as other ordinary demandes, but with extraordinary feruour and perfect constancy, neuer growing weary of knocking at the gate of Gods mercy. The reason why I exhort the Reader vnto this diligence with such esteeme, and affection is, for that albeit God by his preuenting grace knocketh at our harts, to dispose vs to proceed in vertue, and by our cooperation with his ordinary grace we may atteyne to a perfect habit in some vertues, yet the vertue of perseuerance cannot be procured by any merit of man, but is alwayes the sole guift of the Grace and mercy of God. As for example.

example : A man that keepeth
himselfe in state of Grace, by that
action of his, he meriteth eternall glory, but by the same action
he doth not merit to perseuere in
grace to his end, but hath need
still to renew his affection to keep
himselfe from leesing that state of
Grace.

Therefore it remayneth that to
gayne heauen, we must dye in the
same state: and since no iust man
whatsoeuer by his owne Industry
can merit to dye in state of grace;
he had great need to negotiate this
great commodity by some other
Art, which is to pray hard to receaue from God as a fauour that
which we can no way merit of
Iustice. And for this only reason
some seruants of God doe vse certayne sentences or prayers com-
posed of purpose to demaund all
their life the guift of this perseue-

F 3   rance,

rance, with great esteeme of such
a gracious guift, as the last petition
of our Pater noster, *Lead vs not into
temptation, but deliuer vs from euill:* the
which wordes beare a most fit in-
terpretation to demaund this guift.
For after we haue demaunded pardon of our debtes, which are our
sinnes, and that thereby we should
stand in state of grace, after that
we say, *Lead vs not into temptation,*
which is all one as to say, preserue
vs from falling-out of this estate,
but protect vs from all euill of sin,
temptation and other dangers of
the Diuell; which is no more
then to demaund the guift of perseuerance to dye in perfect state of
God his fauour. And thus without seeking farre for other curious
meanes, he may content himselfe
to make good vse of his *Pater noster,*
applying his intention as often as
he reciteth it for any other pur-
pose

pose, or to satisfy his dayly obligation, still reseruing this desire to
begge of God a happy death. And
with this precept I will end the
first part of this booke of the Art of
dying well.

The second Part of the *Art of
dying well*, wherein is handled, the preparation fit to be
vsed when one is neere vnto death.

*The first Precept concerning what a man
should do at the first beginning of his
sicknes.*   Chap. 1.

T HE first thing that the louers of this life vse to doe,
when they feele any sick-

nes

nes is, to caſt their thoughts vpon
corporall remedy, taking all the
care they may, to ſeeke to deliuer
themſelues of that ſicknes, that afflicteth them. And the firſt courſe
that they take, who deſire the ſaluation of their ſoule, is to lift vp
their harts vnto God, remembring
that no ſickneſſe cometh but from
the diſpoſition of God, & therfore
they preſently reſigne themſelues
vnto his will, offering themſelues
willingly eyther to liue, or dye, as
his will ſhall thinke fitteſt. But this
reflecting on the will of God with
reſignation of their own will, eyther of death or life, vnto the plea-
ſure of God, is moſt profitable, not
only to the ſoule, but alſo much be-
hoouefull for the body : for it doth
not only take away that Gentyle
ſuperſtition, to relye only on the
helpes of men, forgetting vtterly to
recurre vnto God : but it prepareth

a

a man to indure his sicknes with a great deale more patience , which will be the beſt meanes ſooner to recouer . The conueniency of this Precept is moſt euident . For that there are diuers ſpirituall benefits obteined by that their ſubmiſſion of their wills vnto God .

Firſt he that is ſicke, is more accepted off in the ſight of God, & ſhall merit much by his voluntary patience . Now hauing thus diſpoſed themſelues, they who feare God, & affect to dye well , they will not ſtay for the comming of the Phiſitian , to informe them whether there be any neceſſity to ſend for their Confeſſour, for ſuch humours are incident vnto ſuch as doe not make their confeſſion willingly: from whence many ſcandals vſe to ariſe , but they preuent the Phiſitians office ; and firſt ſend willingly

for

for their Confeſſour, being well
grounded in Chriſtian wiſdome ,
which is firſt to prouide for the
good ſtate of the ſoule, and after to
make vſe of the temporall Phiſitian, whom God hath cōmanded vs
to honour for the vſe of our corporall neceſſities. But my wordes intend not , that one ſhould not ime-
diatly ſend for the Phiſitian , eſpecially when the ſuddayneneſſe of
the ſickeneſſe may ſeeme to threa-
ten neceſſity , but only for to prepare the mind, & diſpoſition of the
ſicke body, that his firſt deſire ſhold
be to ſecure the ſtate of his ſoule, for
feare he may be driuen into a ſud-
dayne danger, not to be able to order his ſoule after , as is neceſſary ;
but one hauing thus orderly ſetled
his hart, let him then leeſe no tyme
to ſend for the Phiſitian , although
it were before his Conſeſſour can
come : and thus proceeding with a
well

well ordered Christian affection,
whether the Phisitian say there be
daunger or no, the desire of his e-
ternall saluation ought to preuayle
with him, and first to cleanse his
conscience, to the end that all that
shall after happen may better prof-
per. The reason of this diligence
dependeth on this, that euery Phisitian is not so zealous of Gods honour, as they will presently tell
(especially vnto Great-Ones) the
danger they may be in, for feare of
disconteting them, & leesing their
custome. And admit the Phisitian
should promise there is no danger,
which is comonly their first phrase
to animate (as they pretend) the
patients, for feare they may harme
themselues with conceit; yet a wise
man will not trust their wordes, if
any thing trouble his conscience.
because the terrible and fearefull
iudgements of God produce con-

trary

trary effects many tymes to the most resolute opinions of men.

Therefore the more wise & secure way is, to forecast the worst, knowing the most cunning Phisitian may sometymes erre in his iudgment in a matter of great cōsequence concerning the cure of the body. Let those who would liue in heauen, inquire after no Prophecies, but vpon any small probability of danger, let them do that they would not were left vndone, if the danger were ineuitable. But this diligence to forecast the worst, is alwayes secure to doe no harme, & in all likelyhood it will do good, therefore a Christian ought to take that course. But he that is loth to dye, and is not well profited in the doctrine of Christ, will say, it will harme the state of the body, & hasten ones death, so to begin at first, as if the Phisitian had denounced

his

his certayne death. But there is no
piety in this obiection, to frame an
argument, as if Confeſſion were a
preparatiue for ones death. It is ab-
ſolutely falſe, and that he who ſo
ſayth, may the playner ſee his errour, I demaund of him if he be a
Chriſtian, doth he neuer confeſſe
his ſinns in his health? if he ſay yes,
why then ſhould it now be a greater ſigne of death then it was before? It were ſtrange that the remedy of life ſhould be changed, for
that a man hath an ague , or none,
where it cannot be any motiue of
death , but that it is his froward
conceit that will take it ſo.

Another queſtion I muſt aske
of him, whether euer it happē that
a man dieth after the Phiſitian ſaith
he will liue? He will anſwer yes,
for it falleth out too often. Then
how knoweth he, it may not ſo
fall out with him? But if he reply, it

is but seldome; what will it auaile
him that is so catched, although it
happen but seldome? For if there
were but one that were to be catched in that snare, euery man hath
reason to feare he be not that one.
Therfore how can he be so careles,
whose conscience is so guilty? But
now let vs come to those who wil
not make this resistance to the in-
spiration of the holy Ghost, they
not only ought to be confessed at
the beginning of their sicknes,
while they are yet strong to performe worthily an act of that value,
but also following the example of
the better sort, make a new generall confession of all their life, for
prouision if their former confession in their best helth were made
with any defect of necessary circumstances, as are required for perfect absolution. And so for this purpose that diligence of obseruing
the

the number of our offences from
time to time in our best helth, will
serue for a speciall benefit now in
time of sicknes. Wherby the labour
will be the lesse, and the merit will
increase , and the fruit therof will
be very great . Happy shall those
few be, who shall well obserue this
precept , and being prouidént in a
busines of so great importance as
their eternall saluation , shall take
care to put off all impediments in
time , that may hinder them from
passing speedily through the stray-
tes of Death.

The second precept concerning what must
be done about the disposing of our tem-
porall Goods. Chap. 2.

THERE is no man but he knoweth the obligatiõ that euery
one oweth to dispose his temporall
goods orderly before he dieth , but
there

there are very few who settle all a-
right in such sort that their consciè-
ce is rightly discharged, and their
neyghbours well edified. In which
course we see Gods iudgmèts rightly executed vpon diuers great persons, who differring from day to
day to setle their wils, at what time
they are surprised with any great
paine, they commit most grosse errours, because sometimes they eyther are not alwayes in their perfect sense, or if they be, they are so
afflicted with their paine, or so tormented with the sense of relin-
quishng their rèporal goods which
they loue immoderatly, that they
do not know rightly what they
doe, and that which is worst of all
they loose both body and soule for
ill disposing of their goods. To
preuent this inconueniency, those
who feare God, vse to make their
wills in their perfect health, considering

dering aduisedly , what they are
bound in confcience to doe, in e-
nery thing to do no wronge to o-
thers after them; and after to order
what is freely in their liberty for
the greateft fruite of their foule:
That when fickenes feizeth vpon
them , they then do only confirme
that , on which they had delibera-
ted with all due confideration and
feare of God, and then they retire
with all the affections of their hart
to treate to be admitted vnto the
inheritage of the new Teftament
of Iefus Chrift our Lord . But he
who hath not byn fo carefull of his
foule before , muft now at leaft in
the beginning of his ficknes order
his eftate, with the affiftace of fuch
trufty friends as he may cleare all
doubts that may rife by the diftri-
bution of his goods.

Heere my purpofe is not to treat
of ech particular obligation, which
are

are not to my cafe, but of thofe
which are fitteft for my vfe I will
deuide into three parts: to wit, Satisfaction to his Creditours, and to
his Children his common heires,
which fhall be the firft. To bequeath fome thing not by the way
of obligation but of fauour & gra-
titude, to fuch as fhall haue need, to
thofe who haue ferued him faythfully, or done him any pleafure yet
vnrequited, which is the fecond.
To difpofe legacies for the feruice
of God, as to help orphans or yong
maides, who for want of fome ho-
neft meanes may runne a hazard
of their honefty, or for the ordey-
ning of fome Maffes for holy vfes,
or for miffions into new-found
landes where the people haue no
meanes of themfelues to be inftru-
cted in matters neceffary vnto their
faluation, which is the third. Wher-
vnto I adioyne a matter not of an
                                    other

other nature, but of most importance for himselfe, (since orderly
charity should both begin and end
with it selfe) to cause masses to be
offered for his owne soule, to be
quitted from his due satisfaction in
Purgatory. And in this case I can
not choose but lament and admire
the great carelesnes of diuers rich
men, who among many clauses of
their last Testament, seeme least to
respect themselues, since it is a great
likelihood the more rich they dye,
the longer satisfaction haue they to
endure in Purgatory, if happily
they get thither.

Thefe three points I haue touched for a patterne of many other,
wher n I wold not haue the reader
to erre, without reaping profit of
those things which he now must
leaue behind him when he depar-
teth out of his transitory life. And
as concerning this last disposition
of

of his goods he must part with of
necessity, whether his will were
made in health, or in sicknes, let
him repeate often the confirmation
thereof, after his confession and hauing communicated; to the end that
all these actes either of Iustice, gra-
titude, or mercy, that are conteined
in his will, being often renewed,
and willingly disposed, may be so
many new acts to merit eternall
saluation. Because it may so fal out
that though heeretofore he haue
done all these actes, yet being then
in mortall sin they could stand him
in no steed for his owne saluation.
This note is of great seruice to secure the fruit of their labours, who
dispose any thing of those goods
which in their owne life they haue
gathered. Let him take care to be
rid as soone as he can of these temporall goods with a pious intent,
and earnest desire to trafficke in this
                              small

fmall time he may liue, for the gai-
ning of euerlafting life, and herein
let him hold himfelfe fo affured, as
piety and Chriftian prudence may
perfwade him.

The third Precept, what one ought to do
when his fickeneffe doth increafe.
Chap. 3.

THEY who haue any feare
of God, admit they be not
truly fpirituall, as foone as they
find their ficknes to increafe, and
that they are in great dåger to dye,
hauing difcharged themfelues of
their worldly troubles, let them
turne towards God with all the affection they fhall be able. This is
the time that euery man falleth into the hands of God, eyther to receyue punifhment or reward. But
they who know how things paffe
in the next world (as thofe Chriftians

ftians , who are beft illuminated
do) turne vnto God with greater
care, becaufe they well vnderftand
the danger they are in . But they
that are come to that paffe , had
need to conuert themfelues vnto
our Lord Iefus with all their hart,
becaufe they know that in him lyeth all their help. And that he may
apply his mind with true affection , let him with great refolution
abandon all temporall cogitations, for that they are vtter enemies
to the health of the foule . Let him
fet afide the world , his wife ,
his children , and euery ·thing
wherin he euer tooke pleafure. Let
him forget all humane fenfe , and
reafon. It is not time now to thinke
on thefe things ; & to be freer from
thefe tentations , he fhould caufe
that they come not oft in his fight :
and let him do it with al freedome
of mind that he can, for fo it wil be
                                        better

better accepted of God, for whose loue he must do it.

And if it be so necessary to separate those who to the opinion of the world are not to be excluded, it will follow that other curiosities of lesse moment are to be reiected: as are the curious visits of friends, and kindred, vnlesse they be of such persons, who may affoard vs some spirituall consolation for the good of our soule; so that if they be necessary for this end, it is good they should assist vs, as I mind to declare in the fift chapter. When he hath thus absented himselfe from al thinges that may distract his cogitations, let him often call for his Confessour, to cleane and purify his conscience the better, and to increase the grace which is imparted by the Sacrament of Pennance: laboring to obtayne true griefe, and detestation of his sinnes in ech cōfession.

feſſion, as his ſickenes will permit him. And if it be the ſelfeſame Confeſſour to whome he made his generall confeſſion at firſt, it ſhall be well, that beſides thoſe particuler ſinns, which ordinarily occurre, he do likewiſe confeſſe & condemne himſelfe anew of all the ſinns before confeſſed in all his life, becauſe from hence may ariſe ſundry good thinges, and ſpirituall admoniſhments to ſecure his ſoule the more. Let not the Confeſſour be negligent at this tyme, to miniſter the Sacrament of Penmance as perfectly as he cã, helping the penitẽt to deteſt and hate his ſinnes, more for that he hath been vngratefull vnto the loue of God, then that he hath incurred the danger of damnation.

Let not the Confeſſour make to much haſt, nor execute his office for any expected reward, but deale

with the dying man, with a pious
and charitable affection ; vsing all
possible diligence , that a perfect
confession should require: and that
which most importeth, instructing
his penitent to perfect the actes of
true contrition , with the propriety and forme , as the Deuines doe
teach, before he pronounce his absolution. For example, let him not
proceed to absolution instantly after the penitent hath sayd what he
can, but let him pause a while, and
let him put him in remembrance
to performe such true acts of contrition, as shall be fittest for the nature of euery sinne confessed ; and
after he hath confirmed such actes
of true contrition, then he may absolue him. But because euery Confessour doth not alwayes imploy
such charitable labour , as the great
charge of his office would require ,
therefore let the sicke man if he be

G   able

able take speciall care to performe those acts eyther alone, or with his Confessour, that he may leese no fruit of the Sacrament according to his fitter disposition. Happy are they that make a perfect confessiõ, for they receyue inestimable good thereby, which if it do not manifestly appeare in this world, it will euidently be manifested heereafter what worth it is off.

The fourth Precept, of the due receyuing his last Viaticum, and the Sacrament of Extreme Vnction. Chap. 4.

AFTER that one hath cleane swept the howse of his soule from all earthly thoughts and affections, & purifyed his conscience by the holy Sacrament of Pennance once or often, he ought with a most feruent desire of loue, long to receyue that bread, aboue

all

all breades, the perfect substantiall
body of Christ Iesus, as a strength-
ning Viaticum to goe on his iourney without fainting, or wanting
breath to ascend to the top of the
mountayne of God. But there is no
tongue in the earth that can fitly
expresse the great consolation, that
he shall receyue, who shall worthily receaue that his last food; &
although the perfection cannot be
explicated, yet let the Reader much
esteeme to be made partaker of so
infinite a fauour, and let him prepare himselfe the best he may to receyue it with his purest affection:
And to the end he may enioy the
fruit that he pretendeth, I will present vnto him a methode of certaine actes, which he should make,
when the Blessed Sacrament is
brought vnto him, as follow. After he hath sayd his Confession, if
he be a man of wise discourse, that

G 2   shall

shall not haue necessity of an In-
structer heerein, let him say to the
Priest, who holdeth the Host in
his hands, I pray Sir hold a while,
that with due reuerence I may a-
dore my Blessed Sauiour, and then
mentally, or if he can for more cō-
solation to himselfe and the assi-
stants, let him vocally make a profession of his fayth, eyther as it is set
down in the Apostles Creed, or as
it may please himself to this effect.

O my Lord, and Creatour, I
do belieue an vnity in the Trinity,
the Father, the Sonne, & the Holy Ghost, three persons, one Deity,
one Essence, Omnipotēt, Highest
Infinite, wisest, most Glorious,
without beginning or end, withall
perfections, that the Catholique
Church (wherin the true faith wil
reside to the end of the world)
doth acknowledge. I doe belieue
o Lord, that thy Sonne Iesus, the
                                    second

second person in Trinity , did
vouchsafe to take mans nature on
him, was conceyued miraculously
by the power of the third person
the Holy Ghost , naturally nourished in the Wombe of our Blessed
Lady,and borne into this world of
the perpetuall Virgin MARY,
without any ruption of her, as in
other woemen. Thou didst willingly suffer thy most bitter Passion as well for my sinnes in particuler, as for all mens in generall.
Thou didest really dye in thy Hu-
manity, thou didest rise and ascend
into Heauen . Thou wilt come to
iudge al the world, to giue vnto e-
euery one according to his works .
I belieue moreouer that for a finall
Memoriall of thy loue vnto man,
thou didest leaue him this admirable pledge of thy eternall loue,this
most venerable Sacrament , where
(although obscured vnder this spe-

G 3   **cies**

cies of bread and wine) we may dayly to our vnspeakable comfort receaue thy perfect and natural, into our corruptible body. I belieue all that the Catholike Church thy spouse commandeth, and I would rather dye the worst death, then willingly deny the least point of that Catholike Fayth. For thou O Lord art truth itselfe, & thou wilt not informe thy spouse any thing that may be false. I now protest I dye in this profession, and will sooner renounce all the euident certaintyes, which my senses informe me in, then I will make the least doubt of any thing, which thy Catholike Church would haue we belieue, although I can no way sensibly conceaue the same.

Some such profession concerning Fayth may serue, wherein he may expresse his belieuing all diuine verityes, his loue towards the,
and

and his zeale to dye in defence of
them . Let him make the like act
of Hope, saying : O Lord my Redeemer Iesus Christ, I doe most firmely belieue in thy bounty, that
thou wilt saue me, I doe assure my
selfe according vnto thy nature, &
name, and not to make voyd thy
passion, that thou wilt be pleased
now to saue me, whome thou once
createdst for no other end. It is most
true I haue committed many, and
most grieuous sinnes agaynst thy
goodnes, the which if in number
they were infinite, in nature most
malitious, in thy sight must vgly, &
detestable : Yet am I well assured, that one drop of thy precious
bloud, shed in thy bitter death, offered on purpose for a ransome therof, would extinguish the number,
would alter the nature, and purify
the foulenes of them, and wash thē
as white as snow . Heereupon I
G 4   make

make no doubt but by thy goodnes, to attayne euerlasting saluation. O Lord of infinite mercy, neuer did sinner call hartily on thee, but thou didest shew him mercy, therfore I humbly now craue thou wilt impart thy mercy vnto me. If I found my selfe euen at the gates of Hell, I would be bold to trust, that thou wouldest take me backe agayne with thy mercy, & reconcile me to thy fauour, although I had byn the most wicked creature in the world.

I belieue faythfully, O Sonne of God, & my only deliuerer, that by the meanes of this Blessed Sacrament, wherein thy Diuine Maiesty dost now descēd in the mouth of thy vnworthy creature, thou wilt be pleased to cōduct me to the eternall glory. This being done, let him proceed to some acts of the loue of God thus: O Lord God most

moſt worthy of all the loue of the
world, I do offer vp vnto thee the
duty of my hart, with my greateſt
deſire to be ſo vnited vnto thee, as
thou art pleaſed ſo baſe a creature
may be conioyned. Thou infinite
bounty, that draweſt all whome
thou pleaſeſt vnto thee, I offer vp
my ſoule empty of al other deſires,
repleniſh its emptynes, with thy
loue. I doe deſire to behold thee
without the veile of this Sacramēt,
to be transformed into thee, and to
haue no other cogitation then to
attend this eternall charity. I deſire
no other good, but the fruition of
thee, who art the bright beauty of
thy Father. Oh, that I had as many
harts as thy Angels & Saints haue,
that I might haue them all infla-
med with the pure fire of thy loue,
that I might loue thy infinite bōn-
ty, without end. Out of this act of
loue wil follow a more perfect act
of

of contrition: Most mercifull Lord, I repent me from the bottome of my hart, that euer I was so foolish to offend thy infinite goodnes, and now I propose, if I should liue a thousand yeares, I would doe the best I could neuer once to offend thee willingly, only to enioy thy loue. I now detest my sinnes, for that they contradicted thy purity. I hope all the loue of the world shall not intice me to offend thy goodnesse. I will willingly suffer death before I will consent to cōmit one veniall sinne. O Lord, how should I now reioyce, had I neuer offended thee : but since I haue, I repent me of the same most hartily, and propose heereafter neuer to displease thee. O most pure Lord, I accurse, and hate sin, more then Hell, because it offendeth thee.

These actes are the principall
wea-

weapons a sicke man must combat at his death : but these the present Reader may practise at more ease now in health, to be more expert in them at his tyme of need, eyther before, or after he hath receyued the blessed Sacramét. Now may the Priest who all this while hath attéded these actes of the sickman, giue him the last Viaticum with more profit to the sicke-man, and consolation to those attendáts: but because there are very few, who haue such strength and spirit of their owne selues, to performe these acts; the Priest shall do well to performe his duty, and do good seruice to God, if yet he shall pause with the Sacrament in his hand, & before he giue it him, that he say such like words, & make the sickeman answer with his consent at least vnto such actes; not suffering him to loose by ignorance

G 6   such

such an ineſtimable benefit.

After the ſicke-man hath receyued his laſt viaticum, let him humbly requeſt the holy Oyle, the laſt
Sacrament to be applyed in this
life, called Extreme Vnction; and
when it is brought vnto him, let
him be as attentiue as he can vnto
all the ceremonies: and as they an-
noint one ſenſe after another with
the holy Oyle, let the ſicke-man
humbly craue pardon for all the
ſinnes that in euery ſenſe he hath
offended. Now heere let me put
the reader in mind if euer he ſhold
be preſent about a man who is dā-
gerouſly ſicke, and if the Prieſt
ſhould be more negligent thē were
fit, that he be bold to admoniſh
him, for that many tymes it hapneth that for feare of frighting the
ſicke-man, they differ theſe Sacraments vntill the ſicke-man be paſt
ſenſe, & conſequently leeſeth the
bene-

benefit of all thefe voluntary acts.

The fifth Precept, what the ficke-man
must do when he draweth nigh to
dye. Chap. 5.

VVHEN the ficke-man
hath receyued thefe laft
Sacraments, & draweth on to dye,
let him be admonifhed, to make
vfe of fuch acts as will ferue his
turne fittest agaynst the temptatiõs
of the Diuell. And becaufe themfelues be vfually weake at that
tyme, it fhall be needfull to call
for fome fit fpirituall man, who
knoweth how to performe his duty actiuely. Yet the dying man
muft rayfe his fpirits as much as he
is able, knowing how auaylable it
may be for him:and the moft important of all will be, to renew
fome of thofe acts I haue expreffed
in the laft Chapter, becaufe if at his
                              houre

houre of death he do belieue truly, hope confidently, loue God sincerly, and detest sinne coragiously, he may before he part sing a victory; and therefore the best counsell wil be, to ground himselfe in those vertues in that little tyme he hath to liue.

But as well for the exercising of these vertues, as for other acts fit for the state of the sicke-man, a good spirituall man may doe him great good, without wearying the sick-man, but rather easing of him, causing him to gayne many degrees of grace, and glory. Vnto whome I will tell what I thinke concerning this matter, admonishing them of many most necessary circumstances they are to practice, fit as well for the tyme before their senses leaue them, as also after they haue lost the vse of hearing and seing, and are now left to
the

the fingle combat with the enemy.
And therefore in this Chapter, and
thofe that fhall follow, I will chie-
fly treate of thofe thinges, which
the ficke-man in health muft be
prouided off, which may much
fteed him, when others can help
him no more, and the which may
much aduantage thofe who are a-
bout him, to helpe the ficke-man
before his fenfes fayle him; and
beginning where I left in the laft
Chapter, I admonifh, that whi-
left he can fpeake, he neuer loofe
out of his mouth, and when his
fpeach fayleth, him let him re-
teyne in his hart, thefe foure
wordes: I *belieue*, I *hope*, I *loue*,
I *repent*, fixing the eyes of his hart
on I e s v s C h r i s t crucify-
ed, affuring himfelfe to ouercome
his enemy, and gayne eternall life.
Then let thofe that be about him
haue care without clamor or trou-
bling

bling the ficke body, but gently &
quietly let them pronounce thofe
actes for him, in fuch manner as
the fick-man fhall take no more
paine but to anfwere *Yea* or *No:* for
in fo doinge, they fhall not omit
the good they intend, and fhal execute it with that fweetnes as the
ftate of the fick-mans weaknes fhal
require.

Thus let them who are about
him moue him ofté by reafonable
intermiffiós to make brief anfwers
to thofe queftions, mouing him
more to apply his hart, then his
wordes therunto: befides thefe diligences let the ficke man if he can,
otherwife let them put him in remembrance, hartily to offer vp his
foule vnto God, refigning himfelfe
wholy and in all thinges to his he-
ly will, in fuch fort as that as often
as he fhall breath, fo often he may
facrifice himfelfe vp to God; & that
                                    thefe

thefe facrifices of his hart may be of greater merit, and more pleafing vnto the Diuine Maiefty, let him vnite vnto his owne, that facrifice which Chrift offred vp vnto his Father, making an vnion with his fuffering with Chrifts fufferings, his death with the death of Chrift: and likewife let him determine to vnite him felfe with the bleffed Virgin Mary, and thofe Saints whome he vfed as his Aduocats, & after with all the Saints and iuft in heauen or earth: and thefe kind of Afpiratiõs fhal be vnto him a great comfort, at that houre.

Befides, let not the ficke-man forget, to be prouided of holy water, and fome picture of the Crucifix, & a Hallowed candle, burning by him, reprefenting his burning fayth he meaneth to dy with; and let him put about his neck or arme, fome hallowed Medall, or Graine wher-

wherunto is annexed a plenary indulgence, pronouncing if he can with his mouth, if not, in his hart, the holy Name of *Iesus*, and often repeat this sweet Name with great confidence, which signifieth, and promiseth Saluation. I say let the sicke-man prouide these thinges, which although they who are about him ought to prouide, yet it is of more merit if the sickeman himselfe take care to call for them, and preuent with his owne deuotion, the diligence of those who attend him.

The sixth precept, concerning the Inuocation of Saints. Chap. 6.

THE extreme necessity that a man findeth himselfe in whē death doth approach, doth oblige him to recur vnto those who may affoard him any help: such are the
Saints,

Saints, and especially his patrons,
who by meanes of the correspondence of their charity, will now
be more painfull for vs then at o-
ther times. And therfore that he
may proceed orderly, let him first
lift vp his hart vnto Iesus Christ
our Lord, calling on him with
profound humility ; and relying
vpon his bloud and merits, let him
craue his mercy with an assured
hope to receiue it. And after let him
ioyne vnto the merits of Christ
the litle good that euer he did, and
the paines which now patiently
for Christs sake he determineth to
endure , & let him be of good assurance, that he wil not shut the dore
of mercy against him.

   Next let him implore the aide
of the Blessed Virgin , considering
that she is the mother of mercy, &
is ready to helpe those who are afflicted: as is most apparent by so
                              many

many Miracles, that fhe hath done
for finners, and others who in their
affl ctiõs haue fought her affistan-
ce ; fo as it may appeare that Chrift
hath placed her for a means to obtaine mercy of him for vs, being
pleafed that we fhold feek to make
her our Interceffour for vs vnto
him. And in this confideratiõ hartily let him cal her Queene of heauen, and neuer make doubt of her
clemency. Next in order he muft
call vpon the other Saints, efpecially thofe to whome in his courfe of
life he was moft deuoted, and a-
mong them he muft remember his
good guardian Angell, as his pro-
tectour and defender : vnto whofe
charge it appertaines to conduct
his foule to a good end, who hath
guided him, and defended him all
his life.

Then let him intreat the prayers of he Seruants of God, and let
him

him purpose to make satisfaction
for his sinnes, according vnto Gods
Iustice if he recouer, and then offer
vp his death at hand in present satisfaction for his sinnes, and let him
intreat those seruants of God, to
helpe him with their fastings, mortifications, & other pious workes,
in satisfaction of his sinnes. For it is
certaine, that one may satisfy for
another, for the paine that should
be suffered in Purgatory. And to
this end it is very necessary to de-
stribute almes to pious persons, &
to the poore, that they may performe the workes of satisfaction for
him. And although he haue not
honoured and serued those Saints
with such deuotion and perfection
as he ought to haue done, let him
not doubt for all that, because the
charity of the Saints is perfect; for
they haue not their senses so corrupted as man hath, to take disgust
                                    if a

if a man do not reuerence or serue
them, but they with their sweet
nature ouercome our imperfections. For whosoeuer should see his
enemy in that lamentable distresse,
could not choose but compassion
him; much more will those Saints
who aboūd in Charity, help those
who haue honored & serued them,
although imperfectly to that they
should.

The piety of men is like vnto
the morning dew, which being
touched with the beames of the
sunne, sodainely vanisheth, and is
consumed. But the mercy of those
who are conformed vnto the hart
of God, is like the water of the sea,
and of so admirable nature as it neuer respecteth our imperfections to
punish them, but with all speed ha-
steth to help thē, their liberality being far beyond our vnderstanding.
And if the Saints beare such good
                                        will

will to vs, as being fenfible of the
miferies that we fuftaine in this
life, how tender then will the affection of Iefus Chrift be towards
vs, who came downe from heauen
to try and feele our miferies, and to
practice his vnfpeakable mercyes.
For this caufe let the fick man who
now is a fpectacle of moft tender
compaffion, take courage, and certainely truft that his moft faithfull
Lord wil not abandon him, when
he is called vpon in that extreme
tribulation. And let them who attend the dying man, haue a great
care to ftir vp and confirme in him
this confidence of the correfpon-
dency of the Saints with him. But
he that is the chiefe of thofe who
affift him, muft aske him many
queftions, to helpe his foule, and
to apply proper and fitting reme-
dies for his neceffity. Thefe queftions may be, whether he do feele
him-

himselfe to place his confidence in
God, or how he findeth his minde
disposed, whether he seeieth consolation from God, or troubles or
doubts suggested by the Diuell, if
the enemy moue any temptations
concerning his faith, or of despaire,
or impatience, or of hatred against
Gods iustice, or any such like : and
according as he shall answer, so let
him who assisteth him, helpe the
sick man with Counsell, & fit reasons, as in the next Chapter doe
follow.

*The seauenth precept, to resist temptations
against Fayth.*   Chap. 7.

BEFORE that we handle the
reasons, which are necessary
to confirme the Hart against the
sundry temptations of the Diuell,
the reader must know, that it is
necessary in our health to be ac-
quain-

quainted with this kinde of Battel, and wel to cary away the reafon in our mind, that we be not to feeke of thofe weapons in the middeft of the confiict : and it is alfo very neceffary that they who affift the fick fhould haue thefe reafons in redines, againft a fooden neceffity, to be able to propofe them to thofe who lie a dying, fince they are not able to helpe themfelues. Now therfore to come to the temptation concerning Faith, wherby the Diuell mindeth to fubuert the whole building of the foule, the firft thing to be obferued is , by no meanes to fearch out for a reafon to conuince all the obiections the Diuell will propound , but fimply, yet confidently to anfwere cleane oppofite to his queftion . Not wayghing his reafons, but oppofing againft him as if you were talking with a drunken, or mad man.

H

Thiᵇ

This doctrine is both secure, & most conuenient. The security is proued, for that by auoyding to dispute with him, you escape all the danger that may arise from the Diuels suggestions. The conueniency is as manifest, for by thus firmely adhering vnto the Catholike verity, and professing it without discoursing of it, it setleth in one a greater confidence, & multiplieth his merits of Grace, and glory: and so the wisest way to combat with the Diuell herein, is, to ground your selfe deepe in faith, and leaue him to talke as he list. I will here set downe a certaine forme of skirmishing with the Diuell, concerning Fayth, that the Reader may better imprint it in his memory, against he may haue occasion to make vse of it.

The Diuell. What dost thou foole? how, dost thou meane to dye in
this

this infidelity, belieuing Errours
inftead of true faith?

Sick-man. I belieue al that which
the Holy Catholicke and Roman
Church (in which can be no errour) commandeth me to belieue.

Diuell. Why fayeft thou fo, thou
wretch? canft thou not fee the er-
ror they lead thee into, perfuading
thee to belieue that God, who by al
naturall vnderftanding can be but
one, fhall be three in perfon?

Sick-man. I doe firmely belieue
the Deity to be but one, & the per-
fons to be three, and I will dy willingly for this diuine verity. And
it is moft obftinate pride, and folly
in thee, to meafure Fayth by Reafon.

Diuell. What a blindnes is this,
now thou art a dying? Wilt thou
deny fo euident a thing as this, that
one thinge fhall be three thinges?
If God be the Authour of nature,

H 2   he

he will not make thee belieue any thing by the light of nature , contrary to his confeſſed Vnity.

Sick-man. I am more ſure by fayth , that there are three Perſons and but one God , then thou art of any naturall thinge , by thy naturall reaſon . And therfore I hope to be ſaued by my fayth , ſince thou art damned for adhering in points of Fayth to thy naturall reaſon . Wherfore be gone thou authour of all falſhood.

Diuell. Oh miſerable Caytiffe, how haſt thou loſt all fayth? what a blind obſtinacy is this ? Tel me if thy fayth be ſo true , how doth it teach thinges that are ſo repugnãt, not only in one article, but in many? Canſt not thou ſee thy intollerable errour to ſay , that a man of perfect ſtature can be comprehended in a litle Hoſt a hundred times leſſe thẽ he ? or that there be ſo many

ny perfect bodies of Chriſt, as there
are conſecrated Hoſtes ? yet at laſt
turne to the true fayth.

Sick-man. Thou balling Dog,
wilt thou neuer giue ouer talking
of fayth, and demonſtrating by naturall reaſon? Therfore auant Sathan; I doe, and will firmely belieue, that God can do any thinge
that made all things with his word
of nothinge, which thy naturall
reaſon cannot demonſtrat; & thou
lieſt, for there is but one body of
Chriſt, althogh that one body may
be totall in many places at once, as
well as the ſoule of man may be
whole, and but one ſoule, in one
part, or in euery part at one time, as
thy naturall Philoſophy teacheth:
therfore hold thy tongue thou vncleane Spirit, for in this fayth will
I dye.

Diuell. Tell me, how is it poſſi-
ble, that a peece of bread can be

H 3   Chriſts

Chrifts body?

Sick-man. Thou lieſt . Bread it
was , Chriſts body it is after the
wordes of conſecration be vſed, &
it is as eaſy for him to change nature, as to make nature : he hath ſayd
it , I doe belieue it : and for any of
theſe verities I would looſe , if I
had them , a thouſand liues.

This is a briefe patterne of figh-
tinge with the Diuell concerning
fayth, which is ſeruicable at all times, but will be moſt neceſſary at
our death: and you muſt be carefull
not to enter into long diſputations
with the Diuell, which brought
Luther into his hereſy, by curious
diſputing with him, concerning
many ſubtile quirkes of the Sacrament, and the proper ſignifi-
cation of euery word, as Luther
confeſſeth of himſelfe.

The

*The eight preparation which confisteth in
certaine Reasons, to moue one to stand
sound in fayth.* Chap. 8.

THERE is no one verity in
the whole world so firmely
grounded, as the Catholike verity
professed by the Holy Roman
Church, whose brid-grome Christ
is, who is true God and man, belieuing all thinges that he hath reuealed vnto her, as diuine verities:
concerning the which she can not
be deceaued, vnlesse Christ her
husband, being true God and man,
may say false vnto her. And that
we may keep a methode in hand-
ling any truth, it is first to be consi-
dered of what authority he is from
whome first it came. Secondly
who be the witnesses, eyther friendes, or ennemyes, that confirme
the testimony of it. Thirdly the
H 4   con-

conueniency in it. Now according
to these pointes, let vs see how the
fayth of Iesus Christ our Lord
ought to be held truer then any o-
ther morall verity?

The first point being the authority of Iesus Christ, who was
the authour of our fayth; there is so
litle question to be made of this, that
pondering the authority of any o-
ther authour of any Sect, (whose
worth commonly doth giue credit
to his sect) with the motiues that
are found in this first authour of
our fayth; our fayth will conuince
al other opinions, without al comparison. For all nations without
exception, haue euer held a knowe-
ne wise mã worthy to be credited,
especially if he be nobly borne,
and of vertuous qualities: and this
Iudgment of theirs is grounded v-
pon the instinct of naturall reason,
which doth informe vs, that those
thin-

thinges are likely to be credible,
that a man of perfect wisedome,
because he should not be deceaued,
of noble descent, because such an
one will commit no base thing to
disgrace his family, and bounty because he should not deceaue any;
doth communicat vnto all, to confirme that his verity. Concerning
therfor the authority of Iesus Christ
it is such, as esteeming it only morally, and politically, it would
proue him most worthy to be credited, and consequently to Christians must needes make the rules
of his fayth most certaine : The
which he that prescribed them, did
also curiously obserue.

Now the first motiue is his wisedome : It is recorded for most certaine, that he was at first, & is still
held for a most perfect wise man,
not only of his disciples, and fol-
lowers, but also by his enemyes,

that

that would not admit him for true
God, as the Gospells do testify; that
the Doctours admired his wisedome, whē he was but twelue yeares
old , at what time his mother hauing lost him, found him disputing
in the temple with the Doctours,
asking of them many wise questi-
ons touching the law of Moyses;
and after being of the age of thirty,
or a litle more , his enemyes sayd
of him : Neuer man of this world
talked thus wisely as this mā doth ;
besides diuers other histories which
testify his rare and extraordinary
wisedome.

And that he neuer learned
this wisedome from any Maister,
but had it from God aboue only,
their testimony will serue, who
sayd of him , How came this man
by his learning, that was neuer
taught by any? in such sort as the
whole world knew he was truly
wise,

wife, by thofe words of the Ghofpell : Befides the many Sermons
which he made, moft full of treafures of knowledg, & the wifdom
of God.

As for the nobility of his birth ,
there was neuer doubt made that
he rightly defcended of the line of
Dauid: amõg that people that was
honoured among all the nations of
the world for Nobility , and rare
Piiuiledges graunted them from
God.

Laftly concerning his vertue, &
goodnes , all the world confeffeth
his life was wholy blameles , fince
euery man knoweth he had the
crueleft enemyes of the world , &
moft curious to picke quarrells to
accufe him, yet could they not find
out the leaft occafion in his moft
innocét life, to condemne him off.
Wherfore if all the three conditions of rareft wifdome, moft Ho-
norable

norable defcent, and moſt ſingular
vertue, which thinges vſe to giue
vndoubted credit vnto all others,
were in exceilency truly tryed, &
confeſſed to be in Ieſus Chriſt the
giuer of our fayth; it muſt needes
follow, that his authority muſt
likewiſe be the greateſt, not only
for Diuine Reaſons, but alſo for all
humane reſpects, according as the
world doth vſe to iudge of all
thinges which are fit to be credited.

Wherefore from hence muſt
needes follow, that ſince this man
hath preached, and preſcribed to vs
to beliue the incomprehéſible mi-
ſteryes of the holy Trinity, the Incarnation, of his Reall preſence in
the Sacrament of the Altar, and all
the articles of our Creed, not one
whereof all the wittes of the
Philoſophers (who had the moſt
perfect ſpeculation of naturall cauſes)

ses) could euer apprehend, vntill it pleased the moſt Diuine wiſdome to infuſe the ſame into mens apprehenſions, by the vertue & grace communicated to the Sacrament of Baptiſme, and that he ſealed the letters patéts of all theſe rules with his bloud; what other man in the world did euer produce ſuch circumſtances, to inforce credit? Yet let vs go a little further beyond our naturall reaſon, and the experience of the wiſeſt Philoſophers, that if to côfirme his authority we haue had ſo many miracles, which cannot be the operations of men, but the ſole worke of God, in confirmation of his authority and doctrine, it muſt follow, that by diuine & forcible arguments his authority is made ſo certayn to vs, that it may ſuffice vs to belieue any thing for a Diuine verity, only becauſe he hath affirmed it.

And

And this confirmation by miracle was so certayne, that it drew the Iewes to enter into consultation, persuading one another to take his life from him, saying, what shal we doe, *If we suffer him thus to goe on, all men will belieue in him?* *Ioan. 11.* Which wordes of theirs carry that strength with them, and are so euident, as they might haue caused the blindest man to haue giuen firme credit to his authority. For that his chiefest enemies acknowledged, that if he so proceded, al the world must needes belieue in him, & yet they were so obstinate, that *Saint Iohn* sayth ; *the chiefe of the Priests determined to kill Lazarus.* (*Ioan. 12*) (Whome Christ had raysed from death to life) because by the most euident testimony of this miracle, many did belieue in Christ.

Behold the authority of Iesus-Christ our Lord who was the Authour

thour of our fayth, sufficiently proued. Yet beyond all this, it is to be
remembred , that he proclaymed
himselfe to be the Sonne of God,
& of the same essence with his Father, which was all one as to say,
that himselfe was the only abso-
lute God: In such sort, as a man
may hold it an act of admirable
wisdome, to giue true beliefe to a-
ny thing whatsoeuer our Lord Iesus Christ hath taught, only because
he hath sayd it , without searching
any other Reason: the which (supposing Christs authority) is plainly
be proued by this reason. For there
is no wise-man in the world, but
will confesse, that an ignorant mā
(that will not belieue so wise, so
noble, and so good a man, that
should but teach him some secret in
Philosophy, or some other science,
which he knew not) were worthy of much blame, although he
                              should

should anfwere, I pray you Syr hold me excufed, I will neuer belieue it, vnles you make me vnderftand what you tell me, by fome fenfible demonftration: furely this ignorant man were more to be prayfed, who fhould anfwere, I do belieue it, albeit I confeffe I vnderftand it not, mooued only by the authority of fo wife, fo noble, and fo good a man, as certainely this man is knowne to be.

The which is conformable to naturall reafon, which willingly auoydeth all trouble, to demaund a reafon for euery ftrange thing, that fuch a perfon fhall tell them. As if a Prince fhould tell a tale to a meane fellow, were it not fit he fhould accept it for good, for the refpect of him who told it? But this being a Diuine verity, that Chrift hath vttered, (as Princes of the earth being bafe men in comparifon

son to him) who will not cōfeſſe,
that it is an act well grounded in
all reaſon, and all due neceſſity, to
belieue what Chriſt hath ſayd,
without trying it by our reaſon,
becauſe his authority is aboue all
the euidence, and reaſon in the
world?

This Chapter is enlarged to giue ſome
Precepts & paternes to reſiſt deſpaire,
becauſe deſpaire vſeth to ſucceed where
faith is not firmely grounded, nor the
Acts thereof rightly exerciſed.

THE conflict of Deſpayre is
both frequent, and moſt cruell, and therefore I muſt be driuen
to continue my diſcourſe, concerning this point, and it were neceſſary, that euery man ſhould well
ſtudy it in helth, leaſt in ſicknes he
be to ſeeke of ſuch weapons, as are
neceſſary to defend himſelfe, knowing

wing by experience what profit
it may bring, not only vnto great
sinners, but also vnto those who
are very good, to be armed with a
strong confidence in God, and to
make themselues very perfect in
this vertue agaynst the battell. And
the reason that moues me strongly to belieue, that not only to sinners but also to many good men,
the practise of this vertue in their
life-tyme will be very profitable,
is this, that when great and dangerous affayres doe not succeed
commonly according vnto mens
expectations, they reduce them into such a strayte, as they doe not
well vnderstand the danger they
are in, and being inuolued in it, do
not recurre vnto God withall their
hart, fastning firmely their anker
of hope in God; it is apparent, that
they very seldome, & faintly haue
vsed to practise this vertue of cōfidence

dence in God in former tymes, and
for want thereof, euen very good
men otherwise, in great tribulations, especially at the houre of
death, are nothing well grounded
in Hope, and so stand in extreme
necessity to vse great force against
the weakenes of their spirit, and
deiection that oftentymes opres-
seth them. Therefore it is the wisest counsell, that in tyme of peace,
one should be armed agaynst suddayne warre, representing often
to his imagination, as if really he
were in the very danger, which
certainely heereafter he shall fall
into.

  And to the end this doctrine
may be more profitable, my purpose is to discorse in this place vnto a most desperate sinner, whose
sinnes are multiplyed aboue the
sandes of the sea, and that he is euen
at the point of despayre; because
                                    if

if my arguments may be able to mooue such a one, to repose a true confidence in the infinite mercyes of God, they must needes be most effectuall to comfort other lesse sinners, who haue not so heynously offended God, and encourage the iust willingly to abstayne from all sinne. And that I may proceed in this point of hope, as I did concerning Fayth, I will heere present the combat of diffidence, & the victory of true Hope, & Confidence.

Diuell. What thinkest thou most wretched sinner, canst thou hope euer to be saued?

Sicke-man. I do hope in the mercies of God, that I shall be saued by the merits of Iesus Christ my Lord, and my Redeemer.

Diuell. He died to redeeme those who would for his loue keep his commaundements, but they shall be

be guilty of his Paſſion who contemne his lawes , & careleſly ſinne
all the dayes of their life:ſuch a one
art thou : therefore thou Reprobate , come with me to thy torments .

Sicke-man. It is not to late to repent my ill life , and he will giue
mercy who is Mercy it ſelfe : his
Name is comfortable to me , and
yet I hope to haue part of his infinite merits and mercyes .

Diuell. Thou ſenſeleſſe man ,
what ſayeſt thou ? thou dideſt nothing els but offend him whileſt
thou couldeſt offend him, but now
thou canſt ſinne no more , thou
wouldeſt haue mercy , when it is
fit for him to execute his iuſtice on
thee . Therefore come with me ,
thou art damned.

Sicke-man. If I had offended him
a hundred fold more then I haue ,
yet now I hope I ſhall enioy his
future

future mercy by this taſt that he giueth me now, to find his grace, to ſee, & be ſory, that euer I haue byn ſo wicked. Wherefore I aske him humbly pardon, & doe belieue he will be true of his promiſe, who ſayd, at what houre ſoeuer a ſinner repenteth him hartily, I will not remember his iniquityes paſt: & I deſire not to leeſe this houre.

Diuell. This is the worſt ſinne of preſumption, thou reprobate, to liue all thy life as an enemy to Chriſt and adhere to me, & now to thinke in an houre to be ſaued. No, the Kingdome of heauen goes not a begging, to aske who will haue it.

Sicke-man. I firmely belieue to be ſaued, becauſe Ieſus-Chriſt the Sauiour of the world, neuer yet ſhut the gate of Heauen agaynſt any, who euen at the houre of death truly repented his ſinnes, and this
ſinne

finne thou tempts me vnto, were worfe then all the finnes that euer I committed, if all were ioyned in one. Auant therefore thou lying Tempter.

Diuell. Thou bafe fellow, doeft thou not vnderftád thy owne cafe; thou being ouerwhelmed with the multitude of thy finnes, thou doft not call on God for loue of him, but for an abiect feare of thy owne iuft punifhment, therefore thou art my flaue, come thy wayes with me.

Sicke-man. It is true, I haue finned alwayes, and neuer heeretofore repented me of my finnes vntil now that I difcerne it were true iuftice for God to damne me. But his forbearing me all this while, giueth me more caufe to honor him, and loue him, & maketh me afhamed of what is paft. But now in this houre, I do loue his Goodnes,

&

& for the tyme to come, doe firmely purpose all the dayes of my life, if I do fcape, to prayfe his mercyes, & to loue him wholy. For I know one drop of his bloud fhed for me, will euacuate all my finnes.

Diuell. Thou art an Hereticke that wouldeft be faued without good works, where be thy works? For albeit Chrifts bloud be of infinite remedy, it workes vpon thofe who haue done good works.

Sicke-man If I had done good workes all the dayes of my life, I might expect at Gods hands, who is iuft in his promifes, a hundred-fould, and life euerlafting. But fince I haue neuer done any hitherto, I fhall be mercifully delt with, if I be not damned: yet I will now begin to do this good worke, and to loue him, and rely on his mercyes, which are aboue all his workes, that he may find in
me

me this one good worke of true
contrition, and conuersion which
he may pleaſe ſo to accept in this
my neceſſity, as it will make the
glorious company in heauen ioyfull for the conuerſion of ſo deſpe-
rate a ſinner: therfore begon thou
tempting fiend, I hope thou ſhalt
haue no part in me.

Thus ſtoutly muſt he abyde it
out, that findeth himſelfe at ſuch a
paſſe, and muſt neuer be wearied,
nor ſhrinke from him, nor yield to
his reaſons, or ſeeme to be deiected,
but rouſing vp a braue ſpirit aſſal-
ting the Diuell a Lyon. Neyther
let any thinke that theſe are fine
wordes, to beare one in hand with
all, as if they were not grounded
on found and true doctrine. Let
no man be miſtaken in this point,
leaſt that errour ceſt him to deare
at the houre of his death. Becauſe
this doctrine is moſt certaine, and

I   that

that this confidence will be moſt
pleaſing to our Sauior Ieſus Chriſt:
therfore let him leane cloſe vnto
him, and be fully aſſured he ſhall
finde remiſſion of all his ſinnes, &
obtayne euerlaſting ſaluation.

How the greateſt ſinner, if his conuerſion
    (although in the laſt houre) be ſincere
    in all circumſtances neceſſary therun-
    to, may aſſure himſelfe of God his
    mercy. Chap. 9.

EVERY one doth that wil-
lingly, and with great delight,
which his natural inclination mo-
ueth him vnto, and receiueth more
contentement, when any occaſion
is preſented vnto him to extend his
naturall propenſion to perfection.
But it is an inherent propriety in
the eſſence of God, to pardon ſinners, therfore it will follow, he re-
ioyceth to put this propriety into
exe-

execution, and as I sayd, in the highest degree of perfection. Agayne since euery one confesseth, that the Diuine nature is goodnes it selfe in generall, not any particular goodnes, and that the nature of goodnes, is to diffuse it selfe by all meanes agreable to its nature; it will arise that in that sense which I haue expressed the nature thereof, goodnes will be best contented, when it findeth an occasion most amply to extend it selfe.

Now, since to pardon the most notorious sinner, and in one houre to reconcile him into his fauour, & make him partaker of the diuine nature, by infusion of his grace into his soule, is the most ample communication, and execution of Gods naturall propension, that can be conceiued; it must follow, that he will receiue most delight, when such a sinner, by apt disposition to

I 2   receiue

receiue such a fauour, giueth him
occasion to execute his nature in
perfection. And if it could be possible, that the incommutable nature of God might be subiect to di-
uersity of affections, I may well
conclude, that then, he would be
better pleased, when he did pardon
the greatest sinnes in quality, & the
most in number, then smaller and
fewer, & would be better pleased,
in remitting the last, then he was
in absoluing the first. In this place
I could enlarge my selfe in setting
downe examples of wonderfull
forcible dispositions, eyther naturally inhering, or sometimes by
accident acquired, which haue so
forcibly compelled a naturall man
to performe those naturall appetites, as no strength of reason was
able to with-hold them from vn-
resonable discouery of their violet
inclination, procured by accident.

For

For example: I haue read of a great mans Childe, who being committed to be nourished by a naughty woman, who at the firſt ſeemed to haue plenty of milke to ſuſtayne any infant, finding her milke to decay, being loth to looſe the cuſtome of the parents of the tender babe, recurred vnto a moſt baſe ſhift. For hauing a ſowe full of milke, ſuckled the Child with that ſowes milke, & the Child increaſed well in ſtrength, and groth, but as ſoone as he was able to goe alone, delighted aboue all thinges to wallow in the fowleſt pudle, which inclination he could not forbeare when he was a man, albeit it were ſo diſgracefull to his perſon, and to his iudgement.

This one example may for breuity ſake ſuffice for my purpoſe, to ſhew how much more an inheſent naturall diſpoſition is like to

con-

constraine the satisfaction thereof,
since such an accidentall disposition could not be repressed . Wherfore to come to my intention, desiring to treate therof with the most
reuerence that the Maiestical nature of God doth require, and my
poore wit is able; I will be bold to
affirme, that there neuer yet was
any naturall inclination in any
created or liuinge thinge, that euer
ascended to that height of desire, as
the infinite goodnes of God , for
to communicate his mercy . There
was neuer man so trasported with
any pleasure on the earth , neuer
any man so passionate in reuen-
ging an Iniury , neuer mother so
affected with the loue of her child ,
no not all the appetites in the
world cōfounded togither to make
a whole masse of inclinations , are
able to equall the vnsatiable lon-
ging that our Lord God conteyneth

neth in his Diuine nature, to pardon sinne, and to bestow grace, and to communicate his glory vnto man; neuer vpbraiding him for the want of his loue, and his ingratitude, neuer examining the malice wherwith he hath offended him, neuer numbring the infinite multitude of times that he hath abused his grace.

And all this may stand with reason. Because that all the sinnes of all the men in the world, added to the number of al created things, can no way amount vnto the multitude of his mercyes. Of which only there is nor number nor end. If this be thus, for what reason should a sinner, loaded with as many sinnes as he can heape vp, lying prostrate at the feet of such a creditour, faynt in hope, or despaire of pardon, if he be truly humble, and perfectly contrite in hart? Did not

I 4   that

that naughty seruant which owed
ten thousand Talents finde easy
remission in that instant, as soone
as he prostrated himselfe at the feet
of his Lord? Was the Publican dif-
ferred ouer, when he humbled him
selfe, and craued pardon? Did the
Prodigall Childe finde any difficulty, when he presented himselfe
before his mercifull Father? These
great mercyes of God, are not ca-
sually related in the Scripture, but
ordained by the highest wisedome
of God, to encourage, strengthen,
& confirme men, in the assured cōfidence in the bounty of God.

And that I may passe a little
further, sinners doe well know,
that the world was neuer so bad,
but they may finde not only a
Christian but some Gentill, Iew,
or Turke, that will take compassion of those that are in misery, &
will pardon their enemyes, who
                              haue

haue not the hart to behold them
to suffer misery, but being prone
of their own nature, to inuite them
to reconciliation; and where this
vertue is found, he is admired by
all that know it, and esteemed to
be worthy of singular excellency.
And there is no man so hard harted, that seing such a man freely to
pardon his enemy, but his hart wil
be mollifyed, and in that action
will acknowledge a superiour vertue, aboue the power of man, euen
in their iudgements who know
not the true God; as may be read
of the praise of the Ancient Ro-
mans that brought it into a com-
mendable custome, *Parcere subiectis,
& debellare superbos*, to commiserate
those who yielded themselues, and
to conquer the proud.

And if this nature be found in
all barbarous nations, only for that
they haue but one drop of Gods

boun-

bounteous inclination, distilled into their soules from that great Ocean of bounty it selfe, because their soule is created vnto the similitude of God; How is it possible for a sinner to make doubt, who humbles himselfe at the feet of his creatour, and Redeemer, but he shall finde Grace and pardon? *Holofernes* was a wicked sinner, and a most cruell man, and in a word the figure of the Diuell in most of his actions; yet at the Siege of *Bethulia*, seing Iudith that was on the enemyes part, prostrate before his feet, he vsed these wordes vnto her: *Be of good courage, feare nothing, for I neuer hurt man who would serue king Nabuchodonozor.* Iudith. 11. As if in more wordes he would haue sayd: I vnderstand well the iniuryes that you of *Bethulia* do me euery day, but I know not how to reuenge my selfe on those, who

hum-

humble themselues, and promise
to serue my King : & he explaned
himselfe further saying: *If thy people
had not contemned me, I had not raised
my lance agaynst them* : as if he would
haue sayd , whilst my enemyes be
obstinate against me , I will vse rigour against them:but on the other
side,they shal no sooner huble theselues, but I will forget all iniuries,
and reconcile them to my fauour.

Now I demaund, that if the reprobate retaine such a degree of
mercy, what ought the Children
of God, that haue within them the
vnction of the Holy Ghost , and a
greater proportiō of Diuine mercy?
And if those who are moistned but
with the dew of heauély grace, by
diuine participation : what is to be
assured of the infinit water of boū-
ty it selfe, & the mercy of God? All
the pittyful & mercyful men of the
world , compared vnto the infinit

boun-

bounty of God, are but cruell: therefore without all doubt, he who shall rightly humble himselfe, (as it is very requifit) shall neuer fayle to receaue fauour.

But some abiect spirit will say, that as his mercyes are great, so is his iustice very strict, and therefore who knowes, whether he will execute his iustice on me, when I desire mercy. This obiection proceedeth from the corruption of our nature in Adam, feare and mistrust alwaies argueth a degenerat mind; and such a doubt is a manifest argument, that he doth falsely humble and submit himselfe, and so his guilty conscience vpbraideth him, that in due he deserueth not pardon. For there was neuer yet foud an Example, that any did hartily demaund mercy, & would vse the ordinary meanes which God hath left heere in his militant Church

to

to conferre grace , I meane his Sacraments , but he did most certainly obtayne remission . For to demaund mercy , and contemne to
vfe his Sacraments , were all one
to fay, I would be a Christian, but
I will not be Baptized: I will demaund pardon , but I make no account of the Sacrament of Pennance. This indeed would be foule
prefumption , and no fort of huble
fubmission .

But he who findes a difpofition
in himfelfe , and defires to vfe the
meanes, & doth therwith humbly
craue pardon , for his firft comfort
let him affure himfelfe that motion
neuer proceeded from his owne
naturall reafon , but from a fupernaturall Power of the grace of
God : wherefore if God do mooue
him to true repentance (for with a
falfe forrow & bafe feare the Diuell may abufe a man) he may cō-
                              fequent-

fequently affure himfelfe, God is both able, and willing to forgiue him, or els he would neuer haue fent him that holy Preparatiue. And therefore let him argue thus with himfeife: I demaund a thing which I am fure is good, & which doubt-leffe proceedeth from the Holy Ghoft, for the euill fpirit would neuer fuggeft vnto me to repent me hartily of my finnes; and it importeth me to vfe the right meanes that God hath left heere in his Church, to conferre abfolution on me heere, that he may confirme it in Heauen: and I will leefe no tyme to do what I can, and thus I reft moft confident, he will receiue me into his fauour. And I am per-fuaded that he that doth thus in his life, fhall make great progreffe in the way of perfection; & if he pra-ctife it at his death, he fhall find great comfort agaynft death, and

Hell,

Hell, and ſhall paſſe quietly to e-
ternall reſt.

Concerning the ſame confidence in God.
Chap. 10.

THESE motiues in the laſt
Chapter are very great, yet if
we adde theſe that follow, they
will leaue a great impreſſion in
him that will ſetle himſelfe quietly to conſider their force. Certainly it is an infinite conſolation vnto
a ſinner, to haue God the Father
who is bounty it ſelfe, willing to
doe him good, and it muſt needs be
a more ſenſible comfort, to haue
his Sonne Ieſus-Chriſt our Redec-
mer, who hath moſt fully ſatisfyed
for all our ſinnes, and thereby merited to obtayne pardon for vs, and
to haue ſo many faythfull promiſes
of grace & mercy. But if we ioyne
heereunto, that we receaue theſe
bene-

benefits, by application of thofe remedyes which were ordayned for the pardoning of finne, it muft needes wonderfully increafe our comfort, and hope of eternall faluation.

What iudgement may be made of that man, who hauing God the Father moft propenfe to pardon him, and his Sonne our Redeemer who hath bought out our debtes with the price of his owne life, & hauing moft certayne promifes befides all thefe, fhall actually receaue the Sacrament of Pennance, vfing the beft diligence he can, with an earneft defire to be reconciled vnto Gods fauour, and heares with pious affection the words of abfolution of his finnes pronounced in the name of God, by an officer for that end by God himfelfe appointed; what els may be fayd, but that he may, and ought to haue great

great confidence, to be receyued into the fauour of God. Only he may
make some doubt, whether he be
capable of the pardon, for that he
hath ommitted some diligence necessary to receaue the perfect grace
of the Sacrament. Yet this obiectiō
ought not to daunt a true Christiā,
for that not only the greatest sinners are vncertayne whether they
haue full remission, but also the de-
uoutest, who to their knowledge
are not guilty of any mortal sinne,
because it is doubtfull according
to the ordinary Law, whether a
man be free in Gods fauour, or in
some mortall sinne he remembred
not.

Therefore that which is euery
mans case, ought not to confound
ones mind with distrust, who hath
so many incitements to trust in
God. But a sinner may reply, If it
be true, that no man knoweth
whe-

whether he be worthy of hatred, or loue, that is, whether his sinnes are fully remitted, or no; therfore it followeth that I haue great cause to feare, who haue committed so many, and so many sinnes: wheras the other know not whether they haue committed any mortall sinnes, and take care dayly to keep their consciences pure, and cleane. This I say, is one of subtilest trickes of the Diuell, that vnder a counterfaite pretext of humility, he may lead a man into despayre: but to preuent his malice, a man must remember to ioyne Humility with Hope, and a great deale of loue, & a full determination to amend his life, and to do what satisfaction he well can, and then God will say to him as Iesus sayd to *Mary Magdalen: Much is forgiuen vnto thee, because thou louedst much.*

Neyther do I thinke it can stãd

with

with any reafon, to yield at any
tyme, much leffe at the houre of
death, to feare and miftruft of Gods
mercy, which neuer yet brought
forth any good fruit; but rather to
leane vnto hope, which hath proued fo happy for many: and therefore in very morall vnderftanding,
if a man would commit exceffe in
eyther of thefe humours, it were
much more fit he fhould exceed rather in hope, then feare; prouided
alwayes, that he vfe the beft diligence he can to reconcile himfelfe
vnto God. And to take out of
mens harts this fcrupulous deiection, I will fhew them for their cōfort an example, which if they will
well confider, it may eafe them
much. Let them remember that it
is nothing fo hard for one to be reconciled to God in the new law of
Chrift, as it was in the law of
Moyfes, becaufe in this law of grace,

a man

a man who hath committed millions of finnes, and findeth in himfelfe but a cold deuotion, or attrition only, which is as much as to
fay, little loue of the goodnes of
God, but a great deale of feare of
the feuerity of his iuftice; Yet with
this poore proportion of forrow,
let him truly confeffe his finnes, &
take abfolution, wherin confifteth
the Sacrament of Pennance, & the
vertue of this Sacrament fhall fup-
ply the other want in the man, of
harty loue and true contrition; &
the Sacrament fhall truly reconcile
him vnto God, as the Councell of
Trent (*feff. 14. c. 4.*) had defined.
For I thinke there was neuer any
fo foolifh, to confeffe his finnes to a
Prieft, but eyther he did it for the
loue of God, and fo it was true cōtrition; or only for feare of Hell, &
fo it was at leaft attrition.

Therefore fince this laft will
ftand

stand one insteed, for obteyning
pardon of his sins, so the Sacramēt
of Pennance may be receyued to
put life into his coldnes: for what
cause shall he not confide in God,
hauing receyued so much grace in
the Sacrament? Truly me thinkes
it is a most strange thing, that hauing so many motiues to hope, we
doe not rely confidently on God.
Now to conclude this Chapter, let
me draw togeather all those reasons before alleadged scatteringly,
and therein I would willingly the
vilest and greatest sinner should
giue me any reason of distrust. 1.
Our Lord God is infinite bounty.
2. His delight is to shew mercy,
and pardon sinnes. 3. He hath
made a most admirable demonstration of the very entrayles of his
mercy, by the Incarnation, Passion, and death of his only Sonne,
for our loue, and to pardon our
                            sinnes.

finnes. 4. In his Ghofpell he hath made moft ample faythfull promifes to forgiue vs our finnes, if we wil orderly come vnto him. Now let the finner tell me what reafon is left him but wilfulnes, for any timerous feare, or mifdoubt?

Surely, when I well confider this defpaire, or want of hope, I do not only confeffe it is a damnable fin, but I may affirme it a foolifhnes & vtter madnes. For the things which our Sauiour hath done to fecure vs of his infinite loue, and readineffe to help vs, are fo great, and admirable, that they may cōfort the faint, and rayfe to life the dead. The fpirituall mercies which God doth to that foule which recurreth vnto him, cannot be feene with our corporal eyes, but by reafon we may well coniecture, what he doth inuifibly, by thofe outward actions which he did vpon
                                    their

their bodyes, when he conuerſed
vpon the earth : it being certayne,
that God is more willing to comfort our ſoules with his ſpirituall
grace, then to cure our bodies with
preſent remedyes, becauſe the ſoule
is a farre nobler ſubieḍ, for the excellency of God to worke vpon.
He healed the Leproſe, he cured
the Lame, reſtored ſight to the
blind, he raiſed the dead, he pardo-
ned ſinners, with ſuch ſignes of
greatloue, and with that facility,
that they may mooue the ſtonyeſt
ſtart to loue him, who readeth thē
in the Goſpell.

Now let a ſinner imagine he is
one of thoſe ſicke, paſt cure of any
mortall man, that he is to be cured
by the power of God : Let him
therefore preſent himſelfe before
Chriſt, with the ſame confidence
that they had, and he ſhall be moſt
ſure to find the ſame help that they
did.

did. For firſt ſhall the Sunne looſe his light, and the Oceane be dryed vp, before Ieſus Chriſt will ceaſe to illuminate their obſcurity that cry confidently on him, nor euer can that copious fountayne of his grace & mercy be emptyed. Wherfore let a ſinner go on couragiouſly, to demaund of that moſt liberall King, who will giue cheerfully, and let him be aſſured to obtayne firſt pardon of his ſinnes, & afterward eternall life; with the heyres of his new Teſtament.

The ninth precept, to prepare for death at hand, to reſiſt the temptations of hatred againſt Gods iuſtice, and rayling. Chap. 11.

BEFORE I treate of this precept, I do ſuppoſe, as often experience teacheth, that weſe many ſinners do fall into hatred of God,

ſome

fome for that they be not rich , obtayne not Honours , nor are fo
much refpeded , as their diforderly defire, ambition,and pride doth
affed. Hence vfe to arife horrible
curfes , and raylings , wherwith
thefe wicked finners difgorge, and
vomit vp their malice they beare
agaynft God : fo as they would if
they could depriueGod of his own
felicity , and glory . This is a moft
grieuous fin , oppofite to the loue
we owe vnto Gods goodnes for
making vs what we are , & for his
grace, and mercy that he hath vfed
towardes vs ; and becaufe the Diuell alwayes burneth in this finne,
he laboureth with all the force he
can, to fix this impreffion in thofe,
whome he feeth apt to be tempted,
& fuch are moft fit , who are much
afflided with difcontent.

He poffeffeth their imagination , inclining the by maligne fug-
K   geftions

geſtions vnto a harty ill will, tel-
ling them that God handleth thē
cruelly, that he wiſheth them ill,
that he hath caſt them off, that they
are reprobates by Gods predeſtina-
tion, and ſuch like, to the end that
the ſoule being full of bitternes,
may apprehend ſuch temptations
to be truthes, and ſo like a madde
dogge turne on him who ſtrooke
him not, vttering blaſphemous
words agaynſt the diuine Maieſty,
which is the language of Hell,
where hatred alwayes fumeth malice agaynſt God, with vnſatiable
curſings. For which reaſon he that
is nigh death, (when the troubles
of his mind are many, & the temptation of the Diuell moſt violent,
with other frights of death, Iudgement, and Hell,) had need to be
helped, by perſuading him, that
thoſe aſſaults of his enemyes, are
permitted by our Lord for his
good.

good, and that afflictions are no
signes of Gods anger, or reprobation, but rather strong arguments of
election, and fatherly loue: as we
haue seene the practice through all
the old and new Testament: therfore supposing this, let vs come to
the combat.

Diuell. Oh vnhappy man, what
doest thou now, thou art left at the
gates of Hell? seest thou not how
God hath handled thee, that it appeareth manifestly he abhorreth
thee?

Sicke-man. No, I rest assured of
the goodnes of God, which he hath
expressed by so many rare fauours,
he hath done me.

Diuell. Belike this manner of v-
sing thee is a signe of his louing
thee? what a madnes is this, doest
thou not see how he hath abandoned thee, as he hath done many
more in like sort?

Sicke-

Sicke-man. It is false, God will neuer cast me off, if I forsake not him, and I hope I am in his good fauour, and if I shall patiently endure these troubles, it may procure me more grace, & glory in the end.

Diuell. Thou silly foole, what a grosse errour is this? doest thou not see how despitefully he handleth thee, to make thee feele the paynes of hell before thy tyme, whereunto he ordayned thee for a vessell of his rage? leaue of this simplicity, since thou canst not help it. Yet curse him, and blaspheme him before thou dyest.

Sicke-man. I will euer blesse & prayse the infinite bounty of God, who giueth me here some punishmét due for my sinnes, that he may please to deliuer me from the eternall hell that I haue iustly deserued, by being so vngratefull for his benefits.   *Diuell*

Diuell. Thou art paſt all ſenſe, thou wilt praiſe and loue him, that vſeth thee like an accurſed creature, and one whome he hath predeſtinated to damnation, if thou wilt not curſe him, and rayle at him, I will preſently torment thee ſoundly.

Sicke-man. I will loue ſweet Ieſus, with all my hart, in the middſt of all my agony, and I wiſh I had the tongues of Angells to magnify his mercyes: and I defy thee, and the more thou temptest me to curſe him, the more will I hope in him, who will protect me, & confound thee.

This forme of cōbat may help a man eyther in helth, or ſickenes, to get the victory: but he muſt cary in mind al waies to for ify his hart towardes God, although ſomerymes he feele ſome auerſion in his inferiour ſenſes: but by no meanes let

K 3   him

him trouble himselfe , for that he
findeth any vnwillingnes, becaufe
true loue to God, & cordiall praife
of his maiefty , may ftand firme in
the harts of many feruants of God ,
notwithftanding the impulfions of
auerfion , and curfing which the
Diuell may obtrude. But the better to prepare a man to loue God ,
with all his affections, agaynft his
laft combat, it will be neceffary to
vfe in health , the reafons we haue
to loue and prayfe God , which I
will fet downe in the next Chapter: and I will end this Chapter
with a certaine memoriall for their
inftruction , that attend to helpe
thofe who are a dying : and this
it is .

That wheras the Diuell will labour all that he can , to diftract
thofe who are a dying, leaft he
leefe all hope of his prey , let thofe
that affift the dying man , carefully
ob-

obſerue the actions, & countenance of the ſicke-man, & if they ſee
he doth not help himſelfe, & con-
teſt with the Diuell, but ſometimes
breake forth into curſing, & blaſ-
pleming; for that, let them not be
ſcandalized at ſuch words, becauſe
many tymes thoſe are no deliberat
actions of the ſicke-man, but certayne violent impreſſions forced
by the Diuell: & therfore it will be
beſt to coniure the Diuell, by ſome
Holy Exorciſmes, appointed by
Gods Church, commaunding him
to leaue oppreſſing and deluding
the ſoule & body of the ſicke-man,
and leaue him free to loue, prayſe,
and innocate his Creatour, in that
his laſt houre. And by this remedy
admirable effects haue often byn
produced in that ſhort ſpace, when
the acts of calling on God his mercy, in the mideſt of tribulation, &
horror of death, are moſt profitable.

K 4   *Fer-*

Forcible reasons, why we ought to loue &
    prayse God .   Chap. 12.

VVHERAS this matter
        is so copious, therefore
I will be more restrict, and only
choose some reasons among so many , which shall be proper for
euery one in particular , leauing
those points vntouched which co-
cerne vniuersally all men : for that
cause I will not heere speake of our
Creation, Conseruation, and Redemption , or other generall motiues , but I only meane to descend
to speake of those priuate diuine
benefitts , that euery man findeth
he hath specially receyued from
God, and on these I will found
my argument. And first of all , I
suppose that the Goodnes , Wisdome, Beauty, Maiesty, Sweetnes
of God, doe make him most amia-
                                    ble,

ble, and worthy of all prayſe, that
although he neuer had done , or
would do vs any benefit, we muſt
needes loue, and prayſe him without end; the which we ſee euery
day by experience, and euery man
may noze in himſelfe. For when
we ſee or heare ſpokē of any great
Prince that is moſt noble , and
beautifull , and hath a good grace
in behauiour , preſently we find
our ſelues taken to loue him, albeit
we neuer looke for any benefit frō
him , or any correſpondency with
him : wherby we may eaſily find ,
that this motiue of loue, doth not
alwayes proceed from a benefit receaued , but from the amiablenes
of that Prince inherent in himſelfe .

Now ſince we vnderſtand the
infinite perfection and beauty of
our Lord God , by the light of
Fayth, we ought to conſecrate our
K 5   harts

harts to his loue, and honour, although we neuer were to receyue any benefit from him. Now let vs come practically to treate with euery sinner, when he is tempted eyther in health, or sickenes; and beginning with the benefit of Baptisme, I demaund of him, who hath receyued that great mercy from God, what thinkes he, what iudgeth he of that bounty, that when he was infected vnto death with originall sinne, as all others, God hath left so many milions of people in this infinite misery, and deliuered him, cloathing him with the nuptiall garment of grace? Heerein now he cannot answere me, that this motiue of loue is common to all as well as to him, for that he knoweth so many whole nations do perish only by the blot of originall sinne, or els with that and other actuall sinnes, from whence they

they , poore wretches , haue not that means to acquit themselues as we Christiās haue. Now what intent had God whē he beheld him with a particuler eye of mercy , & drew him forth from the vnfortunate number of the succeſſours of the corrupted stocke of the Children of *Adam* , made him heyre of the Kingdome of heauen? Certainly it cannot be denied, but that this preuention, that God intended vnto him , without any merit of his part to deserue the same , and hath not done the like so many nations, ought to be a most strict obligation to loue him, & serue him.

And to go on a little, a sinner well knoweth , that he hath forsaken his grace he receyued in Baptisme, as generally euery one doth, for all that the Diuine bounty did not cease to continue to doe him good , but beholding his frailty .

K 6   most

most mercifully hath ordayned his Sacrament of Pennance, to helpe him to rise out of his sinnes as often as he shall chaunce to fall, and he will please to receyue him vnto his fauour with so much loue, and more, then if he neuer had fallen from his first grace: this ought to be a most forcible incitement to loue God, because this inuincible manner of loue, that standeth alwayes expecting to make peace with those, who wilfully haue offended him, is so admirable, as it may seeme a man can hardly neglect it.

And that a sinner may the more fully vnderstand this singular benefit, let him consider, what he wil say, that God would not permit death, and hell to deuoure him as a prey; they alwayes gaping after him, to carry him, and cast him into eternall torments, in all that

tyme

time wherin he wallowed in mortall finne;let him Imagine why he
was not burning in the vnquécha-
ble flames of hell fire, and at this
prefent when he readeth this, who
hath preferued him ? he muft needs
anfwer, only the goodnes ol God,
without any defert of his to moue
him therunto, who of his owne
nature hath inclined himfelfe to
fhew him this ineftimable mercy,
which he hath not fhewed to millions of others, who died in that
ftate. Now if this be thus,hath not
God layde open vnto him the
bowels of his mercy, and burning
charity he beareth him? Againe if
he open the eyes of his hart to remember how often the Diuine
bounty hath fecretly vifited him
with holy infpirations, & inward
callings, inuiting him to receiue
his grace, and frendfhip; he fhall
vnderftand by experiéce, that God
did

did not only loue him a little , but in that high degree , as neuer yet was found Father or Mother, or any friend that euer deserued to be so loued of any, by any kindnes or correspondency of loue that could passe betweene them.

Besides these, there are doubtles many secret fauours, which if a sinner would examine , would make him astonished with admiration of the infinite loue of God , wherby God alwayes setteth a watch ouer him for the safegarde of his soule . How often may a mã well thinke, that God hath curbed the Diuell, from exercising his fury and malice against a sinner ? How often hath almighty God remoued out of our way , diuers occasions of sinnes, wherinto we should haue fallen , if he had not preuented vs by his grace ? How often hath he auerted our thoughts from such obiects , as would

would certainely haue tranfported
vs from the friendfhip with God?
Thofe mercies of God can not be
numbred, which he doth vnto e-
uery one of vs, befides thofe which
we may take notice of ; which
m ght enforce vs to thanke, and
prayfe without ceafing the infinit
mercy and goodnes of him . And
to come to the poynt of death, whē
commonly the dying man is moft
afflicted, either with exceffiue payne , or fenfe of goinge out of the
world, and leefing his worldly affections , or with any other afflic-
ctions ; what greater motiue can a
finner haue euen at that time, then
by confideringe that he muft prefently defcend either to hell or purgatory , then to be able to change
his punifhment, by difpofing his
mind patiently to fuffer any paine
heere that God will impofe vpon
him, fo that, if he be guilty of any
                              mor-

mortal finne let him hartily repent
him of it, and be reconciled; and if
he be in ftate of grace, his patience,
and voluntary oblation of thofe
fhort paines, may cut of a longe in-
durance in Purgatory, that he may
quickly paffe to eternall faluation,
tor which he was created. Surely
the correction of him that loueth
one, is more tolerable, then the
flattery of him, that hateth a man.
For he that loueth, meaneth by his
caftigation to cure fome fault, but
he that hateth, purpofeth by fayre
wordes to deceiue that he may kil.
Surely if a man confider the infinit
loue that God beareth vs, or no
more but that which experience
hath beaten into his head, as thofe
benefits I haue recounted, payne,
ficknes, tentations, nay death it
felfe; it would caufe fuch motines of
loue, as in the mideft of his greateft
afflictions, he would ioyfully
                              chaunt

chaunt the mercyes of God . And if
he did worthily ponder the affection, the manner, and the circumstances, with which our Lord God
did sacrifice himselfe for him , and
the vnspeakable manner of loue,
wherwith he hath so often vnited
himselfe with vs, in the most venerable Sacrament of the Aultar , and
the purpose, that he doth all this
in the end to bring vs to a ioyfull
end of all our sorrowes, if we will
cooperate with his diuine grace;
most certainely all the tentations
of hatred , and cursing of God ,
would litle preuaile. I do not say
these tentations will not come, for
they are obtruded oftentymes by
the Diuell malitiously , and permitted by God, for our probation
and greater merit. But I meane, the
man would gaine , and the Diuell
leese his expectation , to his great
shame, and confusion.

Now

Now let the reader frame vnto himfelfe a Nofegay of all thefe flowers, the bounty, beauty, wifedome, and amiablenes of our Sauiour, fucking the fweet odour therehence into his hart; firft confidering what God is in himfelfe, & after defcending by his workes, let him be affured, that from fo vnfpeakable goodnes, fuch infinite wifedome, no diforderly action cā proceede, directed to doe any the leaft euill vnto his creature, but alwayes to effect good, becaufe a nature all good can conteyne no oppofition in it felfe. And with this true perfuafion, a man will endure payne and afflictions, as fpirituall exercifes ordained from God, to purify the foule, to fatisfy for our finnes paff'd, to gayne merit of grace, and glory. And admit that the euill fpirit do afflict his imagination with horrible fuggeftions,

he

he will neuer loofe the dutyfull
affection of a louing fonne, & con-
fequently he fhall ouercome thofe
fearefull apprehenfions, to his great
reward , in the inheritance of the
fonnes of God.

The tenth precept how to refift the tenta-
tion of fcruples.   Chap. 13.

I Suppofe in this beginning of
this Chapter, as diuers fpirituall
men do agree, that fcruples, befides
that they are very wearifome vnto
the fpirit , they may alfo be very
dangerous at the houre of death.
For fince they haue their concep-
tion from felfe loue, and diffidence
in God, they auert the hart from
thofe principall actes , that were
moft neceffary for a má to practife
feruently, that in fhort tyme they
do fo enfeeble Hope , that hardly
can a Sicke-man fatisfy his con-
                              fcience,

science, if he lend his eare vnto thē, that he hath euer sufficiently made his former confessions. Against this temptation , the seruants of God ought to force themselues in their life, to despise them, making of purpose many actes of confidence against these vayne feares, to the end that at the houre of death, whē it behooueth euery one to streng-then himselfe, they may not be dull to performe those acts of such worth , and consolation. For God truly knowes our insufficiency , nor vseth he to regard those trifles that scrupulous people busy them-selues with. The soundest & wisest Counsell is, to rest more in confi-dence , then in feare in that houre, when one should not be perplexed with small imperfections, imagi-ning only they haue omitted some small sin , or such a circumstance.

Therfore after they haue willingly

lingly confessed what they can, &
their Confessour hath counseled
them not to trouble themselues
with such toyes, let them take hart,
and be bold on Gods Goodnes,
because they can commit no errour
in obeying his counsell who sup-
plieth Gods roome, remembring
this saying, Better is Obedience,
then Sacrifice, because the Sacrifice
of the old law consisted in externall oblations, but the Sacrifice of
the law of Grace is best offered by
humble, and ready Obedience to
those, who heere be officers vnder
God. Cast therfore away all such
Scrupulous feares, as earnestly as if
they were temptations against chastity, or any other vertue; and permit your selfe to be gouerned by
counsell, makinge your selfe of
purpose deaf agaynst such suggestions, to performe the will of God
more perfectly.

An example of the combate of Scrupulofity.

Diuell. THow vnfortunate man
how doft thou permit
thy felfe to dy, without making an
entire, and perfect confeffion?

Sicke-man. I truft in God that by
the helpe of his grace, I haue done
what I am well able, the reft I re-
mit vnto his mercy.

Diuell. Is it poffible, that fo ap-
parétly thou wilt damne thy felte?
doft not thou remember fuch a fin
thou didft commit a great while a
go, in fuch a place, which thou neuer confeffedft?

Sicke-man. When I made my có-
feffion, I did defire to confeffe all I
could think on, now it being of no
great momét I wil thinke no more
of it, if it only be to obay my cófef-
for who fitteth in Gods place. For
fo

fo he counfelleth me.

Diuell. Why thou fenfeles fellow,
doft thou not finde thy too groffe
errour: if they were doubtful Scru-
puls, it were wel done not to think
to much on them; but when it is a
certaine thinge, which thou remé-
bredft, no man can deliuer thee frõ
the obligation to confeffe it? Wherfore attend it now, goe and examine thy confcience ouer a new.

Sicke-man. Away Sathan, I did
not willingly omit any thing whê
I confeffed, therfore he that gouer-
neth me vnder God, telleth me I
neede not moleft my felfe with
fmall offences; him will I obey,
and I will belieue in God, that he
hath abfolued me for that, as wel as
the reft.

Diuell. Art not thou afrayd of
Gods terrible iudgments? thou haft
omitted many finnes, and many
circumftances that neuer came in
thy

thy mind till now, how therfore darst thou presume to be saued and leaue these sinns vnconfessed?

Sicke-man. God gaue me a free, and totall absolution, aswell for those I confessed, as also for those I then remembred not: & if I should doubt of my former perfect reconciliation, this would be a perpetuall trouble to the quietnes of my cōscience which God would haue me inioy, who disposeth all things sweetly. Auant therefore thou disquieter of my conscience with thy scruples. I know I haue heretofore done my best, therefore I am resolued to put my trust in Iesus Christ, & there I will rest my selfe in this firme confidence.

After this manner a man must resist the Diuell, neuer regarding his reasons, or discourse; but rely confidently on the aduice of his Confessour, as if Iesus Christ in
pre-

presence had sayd the same vnto
him , seeking most hartily to make
many actes of Fayth, Hope, Loue,
Contrition : and because it is not
conuenient to waste tyme with
Scrupulous persons , to giue them
many reasons therfore, I will only
bring two , which may sufficiently persuade, if they be well obserued. The first is, that if one be tain-
ted with Scrupulosity , he must be
acertained , that if he haue vsed cōuenient diligéce in examining his
conscience , after he is confessed he
ought to rely on the more sauou-
rable part , which will perswade
him neuer to trouble himself more.
Because if one should attend to
euery particuler scruple that will
alwayes succeed one the other , the
conscience would neuer be quiet :
the scrupulous party ought to be
ruled by the generall rules approued by all Doctours , or spirituall
    L   men.

men , who do all agree, that after
one hath vsed such diligence in e-
xamining his conscience as is iudged sufficient by a learned and discreet Côfessour, the penitent ought
to quiet his minde , and not attend
to scruples which are accompted
temptations of the Diuell.

The second reason is, that wheras all things which come of God,
are most wisely ordayned concerning the substance, circumstance,
number, weight, and measure therof, it is not to be thought that such
vnquiet thoughts , of often confessing, and recohfessing , that come
out of tyme, and with manifest dis-
proportiô, can proceed from God,
as scruples doe most present themselues at that last houre, that should
only be reserued for a most strong
côfidence in God his mercy. Therfore let the Reader of this, be carefull not to vse himselfe in his helth
                              vnto

vnto the vnquietnes of scruples, &
to such troublesome reiterating of
confessions, which eyther proceed
from a vayne feare , without any
ground therof, or els from the sug-
gestion of the Diuell : for if in
strength he practise to resist this pu-
silanimity, he will in tyme become
couragious , and gayne much merit , and after he will find himselfe
armed, and prepared agaynst these
wearysome temptations , at the
houre of his death .

The eleauenth precept , to resist Pride,
   Vaine Glory , and Presumption .
   Chap.   14 .

THE temptations of Pride,
   Vayne Glory , selfe pleasing
Opinion, or Presumption of proper iustice doth seldome happen a-
mong good Catholickes at their
death , but is the most dangerous
   L 2   temp-

temptation incident to such as are infected with the opinion, condemned by Gods Church, that only fayth will saue them, and that God will not impute their sinnes to thē that bring that Fayth: which if it could be true, he were a very foole that would be damned: but since my counsell is directed vnto Catholicks, whome the Diuell may seeke to delude in their tyme of weakenes; therfore it will not be amisse, to giue some aduertisments vnto such. The reason why this temptation is not so vsuall, is manifest, for that Catholicks pretend to obserue in their liues, not a perfect but a moderate state of iustice, the which cannot so easily minister any ground of presumption, nor yet iust cause of feare of their saluation. But notwithstanding this reason, frailty of man is so great, and the craft of the Diuell is

so

fo fubtile , & his malice fo watch-
full , that fometymes he efpyeth a
fmal creuice to creep in at, & therfore it is wifdome to prouide for a
remedy in tyme.

The Diuell doth commonly
make vfe of two contrary wayes ,
both which are directed but to one
end, eyther by aggrauating a mans
finnes vnto him at his death to caft
him down into defpayre, or by too
vnmeafurable extolling the little
good a man hath laboured to doe ,
that by prefumption of his integri-
ty he may leade him fro doing thofe
thinges which euery good Chriftian ought at his death to performe.
And it is true that fuch who haue
liued with moft purity, and regard
to themfelues , may in fome fort be
in greater daunger to be affaulted
with this kind of Battery of the
Diuell, and therefore it behooueth
them at their death to ftand faft to

L 3   their

their guarde, leaſt in that ſhort
tyme they looſe all that they haue
gained during their life; they ought
to keep the middle path, betweene
the two extremityes, where the diuels ambuſhes are placed : for albeit, that of the two, as I haue ſayd
before, a man ſhall doe well rather to leane to Hope, then to Deſpayre; yet that hope muſt alwaies
be grounded, and backed on the
mercy of God, excluding by this
humble intention, all pride, and
preſumption; attributing his good
workes vnto the grace of God,
conſidering that of his owne frayle, and infirme nature, he hath not
been able to doe any good deed,
or ſo much as to thinke a good
thought.

The

The Example of the combat of Pride.

Diuell. O Happy art thou, that
shalt dye in the fauour
of God, thou shalt presently reape
the fruit of all thy good workes
thou hast done all thy life tyme.

Sick-man. My hope is great in
the goodnes of God, that he will
be pleased to saue me, and that he
will not waigh my imbecility and
imperfections .

Diuell. What thou vngratefull
fellow, what sayest thou? it is possible but thou wilt acknowlege so
many fauours liberally bestowed
on thee from God, who hath holpen thee to doe so many good
workes?

Sick-man. I am much bound vnto God, that he hath not damned
me, & that his goodnes maketh me
hope, he may be pleased to saue me.

L 4   *Diuell.*

Diuell. What an obdurate hart haft thou? is it poffible for thee to forget the obligation to praife him and bleffe him in this houre, that thou art fo vertuous?

Sick-man. I will euer prayfe & bleffe our Lord, and at this prefent I bleffe him for his mercyes, that knowing how imperfectly I haue euer ferued him, he hath not caft me from him, but I hope he will make me partaker of his eternall glory.

Diuell. How can thy hart ferue thee then to treate thus dryly with the infinite bounty of God? Doeft not thou remember when thou ouercamft thy felfe in fuch an occafion of Humility, and dideft performe fo rare an act, with fuch edification vnto all men, & fo pleafing to God, that he replenifhed thee with inward confolation, as thou knoweft full well? And likewife

wise how thou hast indured great
sickenes this many yeares with admirable patience, thou hast deuoutly praied thus long, thou hast mor-
tified thy body with hayre-cloath,
thou hast disciplined thy selfe ofté,
thou hast appareled thy selfe abie-
&ly, eaten sparingly, & many such
rare things hast thou done, which
now will saue thee : therefore
thanke God, and be ioyfull for all
these good works of iustice which
thou hast done.

Sicke-man. I humbly thanke
God that he hath tried me,& now
doth exercise his mercy on me. Be-
gone thou Tempter, for if I haue
done any thing that was good, all
the good is to be attributed to his
grace, and all the imperfections
were my owne ; but praysed euer
be the mercy of God that will be
pleased to pardon my faults,and I
still repose my confidence in him

L 5   that

that he will faue me .

The reafons that ferue agaynft
this temptation are many, and very ftrong . For firft we read in the
hiftories of diuers holy mens liues,
how they neuer prefumed on their
owne felues, although they were
very iuft , & held great correfpon-
dency with God , wrought diuers
miracles , receyued many reuelations from God, and vnions of their
fpirit . For vnderftanding well the
meaning of the Apoftle, who hauing receyued the firft fruits of the
holy Ghoft, and was rapt vp vnto
the third heauen , yet did not truft
in himfelfe iuftifyed , although his
confcience was not guilty of any
wilfull fault: and if at any tyme
they were prayfed by men , they
yet ftucke clofe to this doctrine of
humility, learned in the fchoole of
Iefus- Chrift, & neuer prefumed of
themfelues, but alwais cryed vpon
                              the

the mercy of God. I wil not heere
relate the fearefull iudgements that
haue light on some, which may be
a good warning for vs; but I will
come to the present motiues at the
houre of death, which must be proposed to such as are so tempted.

And to speake of him who lyeth
in that case, it is most certayne, that
he cannot be sure whether he be in
Gods fauour: For notwithstãding
all those probabilityes that the Diuell hath produced should be true,
yet it may be, that at this tyme he
may be in mortall sinne, for that
there be many secret sinnes, that
perhapps he knowes not himselfe
that committeth them, and for that
reason he is bound neuer to presume of himselfe; and albeit he haue
vsed great diligence in examining
himselfe, yet it is certayne he can
neuer so narrowly pry into the secrets of his owne hart, as God can
L 6   do,

do, who is his iudge, who seeth all
things cleerly, and findeth foulenes in our iustice, which men may
esteem faultles. Let vs frame an example, as ordinary practise proueth
true, that one who is to be examined in an Vñiuersity, or in some
Iudiciall place, although the person be furnished with very good
learning, more sometims then his
Examiners, yet he trembles, and
is afrayd, because it may be he
may fayle to giue a right answere to the question proposed: so
man being most certayne that he
can neuer atteyne to so much iustice as is able to giue full satisfaction vnto God his iudge, he must
needes be notoriously seduced, or
els he must needs feare, that he may
be found culpable.

This is the minde of all good
men, as Iob sayd: *Who am I that I
may answere him, & in my words speake
with*

vnto him ; who if I haue any iust thing in me , I dare not answere , but I will in-treate my Iudge his fauour ? Iob. 9 . Which wordes doe expresse such a deepe feeling of the strict iudgement of Almighty God, that they are of force to confound the pride of those who thinke theselues iust : and if one would more cleerly vn-derstand the meaning hereof , let him ponder what the same Iob sayth in the same Chapter . *If I would iustify my selfe , my owne mouth will condemne me . If I would shew my selfe innocent, he will prooue me to be wicked* . As much as to say; God will picke out of my words inough to condemne me. I haue no grudge of cōscience, but find all well in my life; but my eyes are carnall, and cannot see that in my selfe that God can doe , and therfore I dare not treate of my iu-stice and innocency before the di-

nine

diuine purity, becaufe I feare very
much to be ouercharged with his
iudgement. This minde muft he
haue, that feeleth himfelfe tempted
with Pride or Vayne-glory, concerning his owne iuftice; and recurre with profound humility, and
côfidence vnto the throne of Gods
grace, and the moft fweet mercy
of our Lord.

The twelfth Precept, what is to be done
when the Sick-man is ready to yield
vp his Ghoſt. Chap. 15.

THIS Precept conteines two
parts, one of him who is a dying, the other of them that attend
about him. Concerning the firſt,
the reader muft note, that it is moſt
neceffary in health to côfider what
is like to fall out in that laft extremity when the foule muft part frô
the body ; they that haue byn fo
                                        long

long acquainted togeather muſt now be ſeparated . Now is the tyme that he muſt looke to be holpen only by God, and therefore now for a little while he muſt rayſe vp all his ſpirits, calling vpon Chriſt with all his hart , and moſt earneſtly deſire to be vnited vnto him in ſuch ſort, as in that paſſage he muſt force himſelfe to imbrace Ieſus Chriſt, adhering to him with all loue, and deſire , and aſpiring after him with all the feruent affection that he is able . For the bounty of God will not fayle to aſſiſt with all fidelity, and deliuer out of the Lyons pawes thoſe, who alwayes in their life haue put their whole confidence in him : and he will worke in their ſoule the full fruit of its redemption .

This memoriall may ſerue for him that is a dying. Now thoſe
who

who are present to assist the dying
body, they ought well to consider the hazard that he is in, not ga-
zing like men amazed, or idle loo-
kers on a strange sight, but they
must speedily bestirre themselues,
with feruour and great earnestnes,
pray for that soule, with great
compassion and perfect charity,
that the goodnesse of God will
ayde him in that last affliction.
For although it is good for those
that are present to obserue and
marke the diuers accidents that vse
to happen to those that dye, for a
paterne to reforme their owne liues: yet in such a tyme they ought
not only to attend their owne
good, but they ought to practise
that charity for their neighbour being in extremity, which in like case
they would earnestly desire should
be done for themselues, which is
to pray denoutly vnto God for
him.

him . To this end they vſe to ſay
the Letanyes , and the other prayers ordeyned by the Church like a
tender affected Mother , and the
recōmendation of the ſoule, which
read with attētion is able to moue
the ſtonyeſt harted man to com-
paſſion ; which euery one ought
often to reade in his health , by repreſenting vnto himſelfe the liuely image of his owne death ,
which may mooue him to reforme
his life .

They muſt oftentimes vſe holy water ſanctifyed by the prayers of the Church to driue away
the Diuell , who watcheth and
houereth about , to get the ſoule
as a prey, and al other holy and pious ceremonies muſt diligently be
vſed , that may diſcourage the Diuell, and procure Gods mercy for
the dying man . And that nothing may be neglected of Chriſtian

stian Charity it will very necessary to haue ready such meddalls
and graines as the supreme Pastour
of Gods Church vseth to blesse ,
to the deliuery of souls out of Purgatory , that as soone as they see
his last breath passe away, they all
iointly on their knees may say such
prayers as are necessary to be sayd
for the deliuery of that soule out of
Purgatory, because it is a very rare
matter for a soule to goe immediatly to heauen: and if it should hap
so well that the soule should be in
heauen , their prayers will not be
vaine , for that soule will requite
their charity .

And the last thing that I recommend vnto the Reader is, to
be very mindfull to procure the
Sacrifice of the Masse to be offered as soone as may be , because the
paines of Purgatory are terrible ;
and it will seeme a cruelty vnfit-
ting

ting Chriſtians, not to giue all the
helpe they can vnto a ſoule that
Ieſus Chriſt payed ſo deere for: and
heere I will end my ſecond Part ,
and in the third part I purpoſe to
treate of thoſe points which will
be profitable to be well thought
vpon , both by the liuing, and to
helpe to dye well .

                              The

The third Part of the Arte to
dye well: Wherein is treated
of diuers sorts of deaths, and
the sundry accidents therof.

Of those who dye by suddayne death.
Chap. 1.

TWO ways men vse to
dye : some dye sodély,
& no cause is certayn-
ly knowne of their
death; others by some
soden wŏnd, or fall, or shipwrack,
or such like violent accident in
sundry manners ; some haue but
small warning ; some none at all,
in such sort as they all dye before
they expect death ; yet some of thē
may

may be able to performe some act,
by turning vnto God, but others
are no way able to performe the
least act of Piety whatsoeuer, and
therfore we can prescribe no rules
for the last, but only to exhort thẽ
when they are in helth to liue wel,
and to take care at all tymes to be
in God his fauour: fearing those
misfortunes which do happen to
many dayly, that are called sodenly to be iudged, when they least
thinke therof. But that which is
most to be lamented is, that diuers
graue persons in the world that
haue most vrgent necessity to be
well prouided against suddaine
death, because they haue enemyes
that lye in wayte to kill them; yet
these men most commonly haue
least feare of God, of which sort of
people I know not what to say,
since they will be so carelesse in a
busines of so great importance. But
                                    the

the beſt ſeruants of Ieſus Chriſt
who alwayes liue with admirable
forecaſt, euer fearing ſodaine death,
and taking all the care they can to
preſerue themſelues in the fauour
of God, yet doe they feare, leaſt by
euill fortune they may ſlip from
that ſtate of grace, & in ſo vnlucky
an houre their death might happe:
yet the leſſe iuſt, who euery houre
are in likly danger of a ſodē death,
with too imprudent boldnes preſume of lyuing.

But leauing to ſpeake of thoſe
who dying ſo ſodenly can not be
holpen with aduiſe, we will treat
of ſuch to whom God permitteth
ſome, (though but ſmall) tyme to
repent. If they haue no opportunity to make their confeſſion, let thē
moſt feruently recurre vnto God
with their hart, performing true
actes of contrition, ſuch as I haue
expreſſed in the 4. Chapter of my
                              ſecond

second part, and principally let thē
remēber sincerely to pardon those
who are cause of their death, if their
death come that way, seeking by
all their force intierly to loue their
enemyes; let them attend to procure true contrition, with assured confidence of the goodnes of
God : for surely our Lord who died
for mā wil neuer forsake him who
shall thus turne vnto him, and do
what he shall be able . This is the
time which will declare perfectly
of what importance it is for a man
to exercise the actes of the principal
vertues , if peraduenture he shall
not haue opportunity at the houre
of his death to haue the Sacraments
of the Church. But if they that dy
may haue their confessour, let them
make the act of contritiō as I haue
sayd before, & confesse themselus
as shall follow; let them begin to
Vtter that which most shall trouble
their

their conscience, and if the Confessour shall suppose the dying man may want strength, let him presently absolue him as soone as he hath confessed any sin, least differing his absolution vntill he hath finished his Confession, the man chance to dye vnder his handes without absolution. For in such a case of extremity, the confession is formally perfect, although he vtter but one sin of a thousãd, & therfore the Confessour may, nay ought to absolue him presently, with intention that if he grow more strong, the man do perfect what was defectiue in the tyme of his first absolution: which discretion the confessor is to vse euery tyme the weake man is like to be ouercome, & must help him in his weaknes, by often admonishing him to renew in his hart the actes of true contrition, firme hope, and a resolute purpose

neuer

neuer willingly to offend God if
he liue.

This order that I haue expressed in a single mans case, may be
obserued in the case of a multitude,
who may dy together by fire, or by
water, or in the war. If there be a
Priest by, let him admonish euery
one that is able to vtter some one
fault, to obserue the forme of the
Sacrament, and so absoluing them
presently, briefly let him exhort thē
al to determine in that short passage a true contrition, and purpose
not to offend God, if they escape.

*Of those who dye in great payne, and
griefe.*   Chap. 2.

PAINE is as it were a chaine that
bindeth vp the soule to thinke
of no other thing but of its owne
payne, & therfore when the paine
is excessiue, and nigh death, the i-
                                                magi-

M

magination is not eafily auerted to be at liberty to execute thofe acts of vertues as are moft neceffary at the time of death : yet the Sicke-man muft be called vpon to do his beft, and therfore he that affifteth him, muft carry himfelf difcretly, taking great care that he do nowayes increafe, but eafe as much as may be his griefe. And to come to fome particulers,it were good the dying man fhould often repeate thefe wordes : Thy will be done, O Lord, conforming his hart vnto God in the middft of his panges, and bearing them patiently for his finnes, with an earneft defire to fuffer in this fhort time, what God fhall pleafe to lay vpon him heere: hoping therby to make his fatisfaction rather in this world, that by that means he may efcape the eternall iuftice, and fo obteyne euerlafting reft. And oftentimes let him

per-

performe fome act of hope, of contrition, and of the true loue of God;
& albeit he cannot apply fo much
affection , as fome others that dye
with more eafe , yet he fhall not
leefe his reward , becaufe rightly
waighing his great paines, he doth
more in doing thofe acts in that
fhort time , then many a man doth
who being voyd of payne may
better apply his mind thereunto:
befides it hapneth oftentimes that
the extremity of paine doth many
times exceffiuely rauifh the foule,
and tranfport the fpirit with ftron-
ger affections vnto God , then a
man quiet from paine vfually doth
not.

It were good oftentimes to prefent vnto his fight the picture of
our Sauiour Iefus hanging on the
Croffe, that beholding it attentiuely he may vnite his owne paines
with the fufferings of his Redee-

M 2   mer;

mer, that by considering what Christ suffered for him, he may more patiently endure his owne paynes, and reape more profit from them. But he who assisteth him ought to labour to comfort him all he may, speaking words of consolation vnto him, as putting him in mind that his paynes in this world will soone finish; and he must haue Christ in mind, who voluntarily suffered more for him, and therfore he must for a while be partaker with Christ in his patience; that he resigne himself vp vnto Gods pleasure; that he be confident that God will free him from the torments of the next world duevnto his sins, by laying some extraordinary paynes vpon him in this life; that he offer vp himselfe vp vnto God the Father in vnion with his Sonne Iesus Christ in true satisfaction for all his sinnes; that he neuer faint in

put-

putting his trust in God; that he often craue pardon of God for his sinnes, and renew his sorrow for them, and determine in future to serue him faythfully, and neuer to offend him willingly; that he aspire with feruent affection to imbrace, and adhere vnto the loue of God, & to enioy him for euer.

These thinges he ought to intimate vnto him by some intermissions, for feare of wearying him, and as temperately as he can, framing those acts to him, so that the infirme man need take no paynes but only to consent quietly thereunto: and although it be good to deale gently with all weake folkes, yet it is most necessary with those who are tormented with greatest paine: & for that men in their weakenes, and at the houre of death are not commonly so piously disposed of themselues, as is fitting for their

necef-

necessities , sometime therefore a
man ought more to regard the
health of their soule, then the ease
of their body; for that cause when
one obserueth thē to be ouerslacke
and haue no affection vnto matters
so much concerning their owne
saluation, in that case it will be best
earnestly to aduise them, to looke
to themselues in that short space,
although it appeare somwhat troublesome to them, because this short
molestation will be recompensed
with great interest of their saluation and eternall comfort .

Of such who dye by sentence of Iustice.
Chap. 3 .

I Heere suppose that those iudges
do greatly sin , who affoard not
vnto the sentenced cōuenient time
to prepare themselues to receyue
the Sacrament of Pennance, if the
offen-

offender do demaund it, and therfore the malefactour ought to be
told that he is certainly to dy within such a tyme, in which tyme he
who is to dye had need to ftraine
all his diligence to fatisfy his obligation to dye in peace and fauour
of God. And I likwife fuppofe that
the Prieft ought to be well practifed in his office, and very vnderftanding, leaft he erre in fo great
occafion, as commonly condemned perfons haue very great need
off. Becaufe he is bound in confcience to inftruct the condemned,
& to cleare certaine doubts which
in fome cafes may be of fuch moment, that if in all cafes he fhould
tell him that he is bound plainely
to confeffe his offence vnto the
Iudge, he may endaunger him to
be culpable of his owne death: and
contrariwife if he do not caufe him
in fome other cafes to explayne his

M 4   facts

facts to the iudge, or publikely to confesse them, he may be the cause of assured death of his soule.

Concerning this case, the common approued opinion is this: that the Malefactour doth sinne mortally, who being examined by the Iudge according vnto the order of Law will not confesse his fault, although he certainly knew that confessing it he were to dye. I say by order of the Law, whereunto there are three circumstances alwayes concurring, otherwise the accused is not tyed in conscience to apeach himselfe. The first is that his Iudge haue Legall authority to examine him : the second, the prisoner must be charged with the fault, or that the proofe be halfe sufficient, which is as much as if there come against him an eye witnes, agaynst whome no iust exception can be made, or if the one testimony

ny be of it selfe sufficient, or the variety of witnesses may appeare to
equall one sufficient proofe : the
third that, that probation be made
manifest vnto him who is accused,
that thereby he may discerne the
state wherein he stands, that so he
is obliged in conscience to confesse
it himselfe likewise. In this case he
is so strictly tyed, that a good confessour cânot with a safe conscience
absolue him, vnlesse he promise to
confesse it, because it is a sinne to
conceale it any longer, and vnlesse
he shall determine to confesse it he
continueth his sinne, and therefore
is incapable of absolution .

Moreouer the Priest must admonish the accused how to cary himselfe vprightly concerning conceo-
ling, or vttering. Because a malefactour now conuinced is likewise
obliged to reueale such his com-
plices, as he thinketh are not sory
    M 5   for

for that which is past, but are rather
ready to doe more mischiefe, eyther to the publicke harme, or priuate detriment, or if he do not
hope they will mend by brotherly
reprehension. And if the Prieft
fhould not admonifh him of this
duty, but abfolue him, he doth
grieuoufly offend: & contrariwife
the Prieft ought to informe him,
that albeit he be lawfully deman-
ded what companions he haue in
that fact, yet he ought not to difcouer them if he be perfwaded they
will do no more harme, or if there
be no fuch lawfull proofe or valid
fupicions againft them, as in his
owne.

Now hauing fuppofed that the
accufed is fufficiently aduifed by a
difcreet Confeffour concerning the
adminiftration of the Sacrament
of Pennance, I will proceed to
the remembrance of thofe actes
which

which the offender ought to exercife as foone as he fhall haue notice
of the tyme of his death. Firft let
him ftrengthen himfelfe, and conforme himfelfe vnto the will of
God, and make often actions of his
humble refignation, rendring harty thankes vnto the infinite bounty of God, that he hath fo fweetly
ordered his ftate, that by the iuftice
that he fhall performe in his death,
& by the temporall fhame he fhall
paffe through in this life, he may
purchafe a better life, and be made
capable of eternall honour : and fo
difpofing of any goods that he may
bequeath, let him peaceably prouide
for the good ftate of his foule : let
him take care in the fhort remnant
of his life, to offer vp fundry actes
of vertues, eyther of his owne ac-
cord, or by the help of his Confeffour, or fuch others as vfe to affift in
fo Chriftianlike Charity ; let him

M 6 if

if he pleafe, proceed in this methode .

First of all , as foone as he fhall
heare the meffage of the tyme of his
death, let him fall on his knees, &
freely offer himfelfe to God that his
will may be wholy performed v-
pon him : then if he haue not byn
before confeffed, let him intreate to
haue a Prieft , and by his ayde let
him labour quietly to disburden
his confcience, defiring to obtayne
harty contrition for his finnes , and
let him make the beft fatisfaction
vnto all points of iuftice as eyther
himfelfe or the coufell of his Prieft
can aduife him : hauing fo done, let
him humbly craue the Bleffed Sacrament of the Altar if the cuftome
may permit him to receaue it , becaufe concerning this, there are diuers cafes, and cuftomes : but if he
be denyed it really, let him cordially affect to receaue it fpiritually,
                                            for

for his earnest desire at that time
may steed him much.

After this, let him quietly & patiently expect the houre of his iustice, offering in the meane tyme
vnto God sundry pious acts of
Faith, Hope, resignation of himselfe to Gods will, of the loue of
God, of his acceptance of his iustice, of the sorrow for hauing offended so good a God ; but let him
not deiect his hart, but take great
comfort in the infinite mercyes of
our Lord, despising this transitory
life, and aspiring wholy after the
eternall. And yet for that it may
sometimes happen, that a man may
be condemned by the allegation
and euidences, and yet be inocent
in that wheron he is condemned,
and it may seeme to him an iniury
so to suffer wrongfully ; in that
case, let both the Priest and penitent labour earnestly togeather not

to

to giue to great place to that difcõtentment . Becaufe when a man muft dye, it will be a fond errour to fpend that fhort tyme with difguft, contrary to God his difpofition, or permiffion, and to loofe by impatience the rewardes of fo many vertues as in that fhort tyme a man may merit by patience, and conforming himfelfe in all thinges to Gods will. Therfore let him cut off this too much fenfibility, and offer himfelfe voluntarily in Sacrifice vnto God to dye for his loue, becaufe heerein he fhall fitly imitate in this death our Sauiour, who hauing no fault, willingly dyed a moft fhamefull death for his fake, & this confideration will infufe great cõfolation into his hart.

Befides let him remember that he hath committed many other faults, for the which peraduenture euen by humane lawes he might

haue

haue deferued death:but admit that humane lawes wold not haue extended fo far,without doubt in the courfe of his life he had committed fome one mortall finne, for the which by diuine iuftice he merited eternall death of his foule and body , therefore let him thanke God for hauing fo mercifully delt with him , that by patiently fuffering this corporall death , he may difpofe him fit to be partaker of eternal life.But be it,he be either guilty or not guilty , hauing once made his confeffion , & fetled his worldly eftate, let him thinke of nothing but to exercife thofe acts before rehearfed to be obedient vnto God his will. Then being come to the place of execution , let him fix the eyes of his foule vpon his Lord Iefus, remembring how he carryed his Croffe vpon his fhoulders vp to Mount Caluary, and let him call

vpon

vpon Chriſt with al his hart, humbly crauing that he will vnite his
preſent ſhame, payne, and death,
vnto his wronges, and moſt bitter Paſſion; and that in his laſt paſſage he will impart vnto him true
loue, and hope in him, and perfect
contrition for his ſinnes, and that
his temporall death may ſerue for a
iuſt ſatisfaction, that he may inioy eternall life.

Of thoſe who dye of a languiſhing di-
ſeaſe. Chap. 4.

THOSE who dye of a linge-
ring cōſumption haue a great
commodity to make a good end, &
ſo we ſee oftentymes many who
haue ſerued God truly in ſome
vow of Religion, and dye of that
infirmity, doe reape ineſtimable
profit in that time, and keep a con-
tinual Centinel to make ready anſwere

were to our Lord when he shall
call them. To such I need not prescribe any new rules, nor direct a-
ny particuler exhortation, but only
to aduise the Reader heereof, that if
any such infirmity befall him, let
him not suffer himselfe to be de-
ceyued with the fond flattery of
vayne people, who will promise
him long life; and let him not be
troubled to think of death, but that
he labour to make a fit preparation
of good workes both himselfe, or
by the meanes of others; & among
diuers other thinges let him often
vse certaine briefe iaculatory prayers, which will help him to rayse
his hart vp to God, and not weary his spirits, and by intermissions
renew the acts of Fayth, Hope,
loue of God, contrition, and resignation vnto Gods will: and by
these fitts without tyring he may
preserue God in his presence; and
these

these will strengthen his hart, put life into his soule, and increase his meritts, and bring him plenty of spirituall consolation ; & when he perswadeth himselfe he groweth nigh his death, then let him striue to vnite himselfe vnto God by often frequenting the Sacraments of Pennance, and the Holy communion of the body of our Lord, euery day resoluing willingly to depart out of this mortall life to aspire with all his desirs to his immortall state, wherin only consisteth perfect repose. Let him read, or cause to be read vnto him some spirituall bookes, feeding and nourishing his soule with that diet, that his soule may be fatned, the more that his body consumeth. Concerning his goods he must by disposing them to other mens vses, free his cogitations of them, that he may only attend to arme himselfe with spiritu-

all

all armour, to be able to refift the laft temptations of the Diuell, and faften himfelfe vnto Iefus Chrift in the laft houre of his death.

Of thofe who dye in the Warre.
Chap. 5.

BEFORE I can inftruct Soldiers what they fhould doe at their death, I need to lay for a fure ground that the Warre be iuft in their confcience, that they may the bolder expofe themfelues to death; yet I dare not fay that euery one who will thinke he doth well, hath a good confcience, becaufe diuers Infidells perfwade themfelues they doe well, when they make warre vpon the Chriftians. Therefore my fpeach aymeth at fuch Catholikes, who hauing good and pious Kings, on whome morally they may rely, and thereupon they pre-

presume the cause is iust, and they carry the minde to giue ouer the warre if they could think the cause were not iust. These men therfore hauing no scruple in their consciences, if they retayne the feare of God in their harts, should before they enter into the battell, do that which they would do if they lay a dying instantly; and the more carefull ought they to vse this preuenting diligence, because it is most likely that in the confusion of a battell they cãnot be able to performe those acts of vertue, or contrition, and prepare for the Iudgement of God which they are to expect. Because a Souldier resoluing not to dye, but striuing by all violent meanes to escape with life, is more likely at that time to giue the raines to audacity, and fury, then to humility, and to craue pardon of his sinnes.

Wher-

Wherefore before he betaketh
himselfe to his weapons , (besides
his true confession and detestation
of his sinnes, with purpose neuer
willingly to offéd God any more)
he ought to performe the acts of
Fayth, of Hope, of the loue of
God, purifying his affectiõs in that
he goeth about , wishing to get
the victory without bloudshed if
it were possible; and purposing his
intention for defence of right , he
fighteth the battell to repell iniustice, wherein it may be both lawfull and meritorious to lay downe
his life : as for other matters, it is to
little purpose that I treate of al par-
ticulars, but it sufficeth to admonish
the Confessours, that they be faithfull in their office, to instruct them
in what manner they may venter
their liues , without preiudice of
their soules, that they liue free from
sinne, that they recommend themselues

felues vnto God, and may remember to offer many acts of vertue vnto God, euen in that fhort tyme when they lye hurt, and mangled on the ground, trampled ouer by the teete of horfes, void of all other help, but what the grace and mercy of God fhall affoard, or their owne pious difpofition, and conftant cooperation with Gods will may obtayne at his hand: and therfore they had great need ferioufly to implore the ayde of Iefus Chrift at that tyme.

Of thofe who dye of feare, and frightings.
Chap. 6.

IT is a hard matter to refolue what happeneth to fuch after death, by the outward accidents which men do fee, and therfore I would aduife the Reader not to paffe his iudgement rafhly, but

leaue

leaue them vnto God, vnto whom
they be no fuch fecrets, & he ren-
dreth to euery one according vnto
his workes. For it hath byn obſerued, that diuers wicked men in
their liues, and heretikes, and infidells, haue at the houre of their
death expreſſed ſo great tranquility
of mind, that in the iudgement of
men it appeared very admirable; &
on the other ſide diuers feruants of
God, whoſe life ſeemed irrepre-
henſible, at the houre of death haue
been afflicted with horrible viſi-
ons : therfore it is no ſure argumēt
by the outward forme of their
death, to frame a reſolution what is
become of them after their paſſage
hence. But although it be a good
rule not to cenſure of the ſtate of
the dead-man by theſe tokens that
happen ordinarily to men of all
ſorts of life; yet when God doth
manifeſt heere vnto vs by ſome ex-

tra-

traordinary certitude the condition of some, it is good for our own profit, to take notice of Gods extraordinary example, that at some mans death he is willing to giue vs a liuing testimony of their future state after their death.

To this purpose we read in *Saint Gregory* in the fourth booke of his *Dialogues, 46. Chap.* of a man called *Crysorius* who hauing byn a proud, Couetous, and Luxurious man, at the houre of his death did behold certaine vgly blacke men to be very busy about him, to draw him presently away to hell. But the man in a deadly sweat begā to cry out for a Sonne of his who was a monke called *Maximus*, to come & help him in that trouble; and the fright was so terrible, that he neuer ceased tumbling vp and downe, to turne his sight from them, yet being no way able to be freed from
them,

them; at the last in a terrible agony
he cryed out a loud & demaunded
respit but vntill next day: but they
would not permit it him, and so in
that horrible perplexity he dyed.

The same Saint also recounteth
how a certaine religious man who
in his life made outward shew of a
good man, and was so held of o-
thers, but inwardly was other thē
he seemed outwardly, and feygned
strictly to fast with his religious
brethren, when in secret he would
eate meate: When he was nigh
his death, he called all his fellowes
vnto him, who expecting to heare
from him some rare counsell, that
might be profitable for them to follow, God did inforce him to vtter
to his owne shame, the terrible
fright and horrour which he endured, for that he saw an vgly Dragon, who with his tayle seemed to
bind his knees and feet, and put his
    N   mouth

mouth to draw out his soule that
way. And he had no sooner manifested that vgly vision, but instantly dyed .

These extraordinary cases wherin these were not admitted to pennance , ought to be our ordinary
warnings , that we be prepared
while there is tyme of mercy, least
we be damned in the time of iudgment : but in the other ordinary
cases,a quiet or an vnquiet death be
no certayne arguments to know
the state of a man after his death:
because a good man sometymes at
his death who is in Gods fauour,
may be permitted to indure extreme torments , wherby it pleaseth God by that meanes to purify
his imperfections in this life, the
sooner to bring him to his glory in
the next . But when a man is thus
affrighted with visions, or molested
with temptations, a good-man at
that

that time muſt call ſtrongly on Ieſus Chriſt, & with great affectiō repoſe ſure cōfidence in God, & thoſe who are about him muſt caſt holy water , which many tymes will driue away the Diuell : they muſt bid the dying-man be of courage, ſtrong in fayth , firme in hope, remember him of the ſtrong reaſons he hath to truſt in God, the Saints will be interceſſours for him, but eſpecially his Angell Gardian, who all his life hath protected him, will now pleade hard vnto God for him, that he may in this his laſt conflict obtayne the Victory of his troubleſome enemies ; that he muſt confide in Ieſus-Chriſt, that the Diuells eager temptations are no ſignes that God hath forſaken him, but may ſerue him for occaſions of merit, & to purge his ſinns, that he may the ſooner enioy the perfect fruition of God.

Of

Of some who dye with great consolation.
Chap. 7.

AS I fayd in the laft Chapter
that the outward forme of
dying is not a certayne rule vn-
doubtedly of the ftate of the dead-
man; yet when a man who hath e-
uidently liued wickedly, dyeth a-
parantly defperate, or it pleafeth
God to detect at death the hypocri-
fy of a conterfayte holy man, their
publike defperate conclufions may
ferue for motiues to vs by confideration of their miferable eftate, to
fecure our owne. So likewife whē
a pious manner of death, fhall accompany a perpetual vertuous life,
we ought not to neglect fuch a
patterne, but take great incourage-
ment to our felues in the courfe of
vertue. To which end we may obferue that it doth often happen that
                                    diuers

diuers seruants of Christ especially
such who haue spent their life vnder obedience of some spirituall
rule, and practice of great mortification, at the houre of death, or a
little before, haue inioyed so infinite consolation, as it may appeare
that God hath giuen them a tast in
this life of the eternall ioyes they
shall enioy immediatly : and their
liuely confidence in Gods mercies,
and their outward testification of a
good conscience, may be a comfor-
fortable incouragemēt to vs to indure patiently in this world great
labours, breakings of our owne
wills, sicknes, or any other crosses,
or molestations, when we behold-
afore our own eyes, one as infirme
as our selues, to reape such infinite
consolation in this life, & to march
before vs so confidently to his most
desired Countrey.

At such a tyme may a worldly
frayle

frayle creature euidently behold
what correspondence is betweene
the immortall, Glorious, & triumphant Saints of heauen, with the
mortall, miserable, and militant
creatures on earth , which the article of the Communion of Saints
doth enioyne vs to belieue faythfully; but especially how faythfull
Christ is of his promises, when he
will gather togeather the prey of
those soules which he purchased
with the price of his precious blod,
seeming to say in this life vnto thē:
Come yee Blessed Sonnes of my
Father, take possession of the Inheritáce I haue purchased for you,
some, we will liue eternally heere
as brothers. *S. Gregory* recounteth in
his fourth booke of *Dialogues* 47.
Chapter, how a Priest called *Vrsinus*
who had liued with most rare example of Chastity , and other vertues, at the houre of his death , began

gan

gan with excessiue expression of
ioy to cry out a loud: Welcome,
welcome my Lords, you are most
hartily welcome to me. How may
yee vouchsafe to come to me your
meanest seruant? I come, I will
come, I thanke you. And the stan-
ders by, demaunding to whome he
spake, he answered: Do you not
see the chiefe Apostles *Peter*, and
Paul are heere? And turning againe
to those Saints he ioyfully cryed,
Behold I come, behold I come, &
with those wordes in his mouth he
dyed.

The same *S. Gregory* recounteth
that a good man named *Seruulus*,
that for many yeares had exercised
great patience through the intollerable payne of the palsey, and earnestly praysed God in the midst of
his griefe, at the houre of his death
called vnto him certayne pilgrimes
whome he lodged, and imparted

vnto

vnto thē of the almes which were giuen to him, he intreated them to sing some Psalmes with him, & as they were singing togeather , he sayd sodenly vnto them: Hold, do you not heare the musike in heauen ? and setling himselfe to listen vnto the prayses of God which sounded in heauen , being drawne and rauisht with the force of that melody , his soule departed out frō his body, and left the roome perfumed with most delicious odours, in token of his most happy estate he was taken vnto.

These outward signes in confirmation of the secret truth, are very rare : yet the inward consolations which such mē sensibly feele who spend their life innocently, are not rare : for they doe very often find such pleasing spirituall delights, as causeth them earnestly to long to depart from their body, which hindreth

dereth them from their resting place,
where eternally they may enioy
their eternall good, which they
haue euer loued, and sought after
with all their power. Such as dye
thus, haue no need of counsell, but
we all haue need to propose vnto
our selues their actions for our
lessons; for euery day they do most
noble actes of Hope, and Loue of
God, and are able to animate those
who conuerse with them, to loue
& serue our Lord Iesus Christ.

*Of the particuler Iudgement of the
Soule.* Chap. 8.

AS soone as euer the soule is
departed out of the body, in
that instant and in that place, it receiueth its particuler sentence, eyther to be receyued into the ioyes
of heauen immediatly, or to be re-
ferred ouer for a tyme to make iust
N 5   satis-

satisfaction in the paines of Purgatory, or into the prison of Limbus for vnbaptized infants who neuer committed actuall sinne, but are guilty only of originally sinne, wherfore they may not enter into heauen vnlesse they had euacuated their originall sinne by the water of the Sacrament of Baptisme; or finally eternally to be dāned in hell. The reason heerof is manifest, that since the soules must be carryed to the place ordayned fit for their desert, the iudgement must needes go before, becaufe their miffion is an execution of the sentence pronoūced on them; and it is Chrift who muft giue the sentence, and it is intimated and made knowne vnto the soules in the very article of their death; not so, as if Chrift muft appeare to euery particuler soule, but by the power of Chrift, who giuing knowledge to euery mans vnder-

vnderstanding, maketh euery soule
perfectly to know, to which of
those 4. places, or to what degree
of reward, or what kind of punishment euery one is adiudged.

Now wheras *Abulensis* vpon the
24. of *S. Matthew*, and *Soms* in his
fourth, distinction 45. speake of certayne particuler Iudgements that
are made before the soule depart
from the body, that is to be vnderstood of some extraordinary di-
scussion ordayned by Gods mercifull prouidence for the instruction
of the liuing ; that they vnderstanding therby the strict rigour of
Gods iudgements , they and we
might be admonished to liue more
warily, and more holily : but the
diffinitiue sentence of those discus-
sions was at the point of the soules
leauing the body. In which sense
a man may truly affirme, that in
some extraordinary case, the sen-
N 6   tence

tence may be giuen by the particuler prouidéce of God before death, as was on some that were cast aliue into hell, *Num.* 16.

But from this which is sayd of the ordinary particuler iudgement of the soule at the instant of its separation from the body, it doth follow, that those who are praying about the dying body do often obserue the countenance of the sickman, doubting whether he be throughly dead or no, or whether the iudgement be passed, and the soule be sent to his due place. For this point no wiser Counsell can be giuen, then to liue well and holily, and whilest tyme serueth heere, to negotiate carefully for this busines of so great importance. The life passeth in a moment, and death stealeth on vs like a thiefe. Blessed shall they be, who shall be found prepared for the wedding of

the

the Lambe of God. Blessed are the
dead that dye in the grace and fauour of our Lord, because that day
which to Sinners will be the beginninge of eternall payne, will
proue to the good the birth day of
eternall life.

Of the confideration of the death of a finner. Chap. 9.

MY intention being to treat
of the fower last necessary
remembrances, which are the fittest
meanes to reforme mans life, and
consequently to dye well; I thinke
it necessary first of all to treat of
death, not by the way of speculation, only imagininge what vseth
to happen to dying men, but by a
certayne meanes which may touch
the affection, that we may helpe
the liuinge. I will begin with the
nature of the death of a finner, setting

ting to view the state and daunger that a sinner will finde himselfe in at that pinch, as may probably be gathered out of ancient stories, & latter accidents. Certainly he who in the course of his life hath contemned the law of God, and made himselfe a slaue to vice, and neuer tooke care to prouide for his end, he is like to vse such wordes:

Behold into what a strayt am I now brought, vnhapy man that I am! Now I finde my selfe ready to be swallowed by the waues of the sea, to the infinite confusion of my soule! I haue liued like a fatt bull, running wildly through the medowes of worldly vanityes, neuer denying my senses and appetites what they affected. I neuer thought on my death: I made my selfe drunke with the pleasures of the earth, as if there had byn no God to serue, and that I should neuer

uer fall into his iuftice. Oh how doth forrow & feare now inuirone me, and I can finde none who wil defend me! My finnes that I committed with idle delight, now like furious Lyons affright me with feare and horrour of eternall punifhment. My owne confcience agaynft which moft willfully I oppofed, repelling the diuine infpirations which by meanes of my confcience did often fpeake vnto me, now is turned to be my accufer, and doth wound my hart and foule with prickinges, and adiudgeth me worthy of the torments of Hell.

The Diuells whom I ferued more obfequioufly then my God, they now terrify me with vgly vifions, and bayte me like mad dogs ready to deuoure me. My Iudge whom I defpifed doth now brandifh the fword of his iuftice ouer

my

my head , and the terrour of his
countenance now maketh me to
tremble. Oh how true do I now
finde , that a naughty man in the
houre of his death will be fettered
in his owne finns! If I look back on
my life , my owne workes cry out
agaynft my fafety, without hope
of any the leaft eafe . If I confider
my prefent ftate, my foule hath
put on fuch an habit of finne , that
fhe knoweth not how to turne to
God, and fhe feemeth to be conuerted into that obduracy , that the
damned fpirits beare againft God.
If I thinke on the time to come,
the life that I haue lead can predu-
ce no hope , but begetteth in me
an infernall defpaire of euer being
faued: and all arguments that I can
frame, conclude I am a flaue, condemned to the perpetuall bondage
of the eternall prifon. I prefumed
in the vayne helpes of the world
which

which I loued, wherin I meant to
eternize my name . I neuer would
treate of the eternall goodes , and
therfore Despaire doth cruelly affault me on one side , and the losse
of my worldly goods which I doted on , and purposed to haue inioyed them for euer, now they
torment me to part from them .
Oh Death how bitter art thou to
me! who shal help me at this time!

This is the sense, and these are
the affectiōs of sinners at the houre
of their death, the which if they
seeme full of discomfort , & sadnes
when they are but written , or
thought on , a man is not able truly to apprehend what it is when it
is really tryed . For euen as the liuing haue no experiēce of dyinge,
so can they not attaine to the true
feeling of these desolations, and
circumstances, vntill they are in
them. For admit a man may write,
speake,

speake, or thinke in some competét
proportion of these thinges that
will happen at that time, still let
the reader passe on further, and belieue there will be more thé he can
thinke on . When a Malefactour is
brought to the place of execution,
and beholdeth the manner of his
death, he will feele a new kind of
affection , and a sense that will
more afflict him beyonde all the
beholders that stand present only
with the affection of cópassion, although they be either Pastour, Father, Mother , or any other friend,
because there is great oddes betweene passion , and compassion;
although some Saints by the super-
naturall power of Gods grace, haue
found the sense of compassion of
other sinners state, far to exceed the
sense of the sufferinge of torments
in their owne bodies, or the paines
that ordinarily malefactours feele,
                                    when

when they dye by Iustice.

But thofe thinges are rare, and
caufed by fupernaturall grace, not
by humane affection, and therfore
they do not contradict the ordinary doctrine. What fury will the
Diuells practice vpon that veffell
of Gods wrath, to lay hold of that
miferable foule, and to proclayme
their victory? what comotion will
that body feele, that muft for euer
remayne in Hell? How will the
foule quake to go forth, and trem-
bling at the hideous roring Lyons,
who ftand gaping to fwallow it?
how loath will the foule be to be
feparated from that body, which it
did fo fondly delight in, to be caft
into hellifh obfcurity, and to be
eternally tormented? *Balthafar* the
Chaldean Kinge neuer had fo cleare
notice of the ftate he found himfelfe in, when he celebrated that
great banquet with his Lords, as
hath

hath a finner who findeth himfelfe nigh death. Yet when he faw but a hand , that feemed to write the fentence of his death on the wall, not examining who writ it , only but feeing the wordes , he began fo to be troubled , as the Scripture fayth his contenance was prefently changed , and his thoughts did trouble him , the ioyntes of his reynes were diffolued, & his knees knocked one the other; which defcription doth expreffe a great feare and horrour of death , the which that very night furprifed him , by the hand of *Darius* King of the *Medes.*

Behold here a mighty Emperour in the midft of his Lords and friendes , by feing a hand he knew not of whom , write a few wordes on the wall, fall into fuch an agony,that in an inftant he was cleane changed in countenance , and his

ioyn-

ioyntes diſſolued, cried out moſt
furiouſly ; being not able to ſuffer
the horrour he felt. What will a
ſinner do, who is not now mery at
a banquet, but deiected with infinite ſadnes & deſpaire; not accom-
panied with potent friendes, but
enuironed with Diuells, and op-
preſt with his ſinnes, and aſtoni-
ſhed at the Iudgement of God, vn-
derſtāding his own miſery, & ſeing
himſelfe inſtantly to be carried
away for Gods iuſtice to be executed on him: yet ſinners will neuer
vnderſtand this leſſon.

The Rich Glotton would not
thinke on this, and take compaſ-
paſſion of *Lazarus*, but did ſwill in
the pleaſures of the world, as if be
ſhould liue euer : but he was violently haled from them, & buried
in Hell. The rich-mā that thought
to ſtore vp ſo much riches for ſo
many yeares, and delight himſelfe
in

in them, he would not thinke of
this, but it was fayd vnto him:
Thou foole, This night thou fhalt
dye. And now in thefe dayes there
are many Rich Glottons, Fooles,
who will not be moued with the
wordes of the Gofpell, where thefe
examples were written for our inftruction, no more, then if Iefus
Chrifts wordes were lyes. The obdurate finner doth more ftudy
how to fatisfy his appetites, and to
take vayne and fenfuall delights
of his temporall profperity, then
he thinkes on God his iuftice to
come. But when he leaft thinkes
theron, death entreth in at his gol-
den gates, and paffeth through his
chambers, and withdrawing-châ-
bers, all behunge with the goods
of the poore violently taken from
them, and entring in priuily into
his bed-chamber, giueth him fuch
a deadly woûd as all the medicines
                                     of

of the world can neuer cure. In
vaine he troubleth himfelfe to call
vpon his friendes, and his riches,
to take hold of his temporal fword,
or glory of his houfe, he defireth
to hold faft his worldly goodes,
which are the Idolls he did adore,
in which he put his vaine hope.

But all thefe will not ferue.
For it is written, when he dies he
fhall not take all with him, nor his
glory fhall defcend with him. Oh
great folly vnworthy of one who
profeffeth the fayth of Iefus Chrift!
I know not what they can fay to
this ftupidity! For Chriftians efpecially the grauer fort of them, and
who for that caufe commit the greater fault, cannot deny the griefe
that thefe their Idols will caufe
them at their death, and yet it is a
hard matter to finde one, that will
liue in the feare of God, and doth
pioufly prouide for his death. But
the

the houre will shortly come, and then will they learne to their cost, how terrible a matter it will be to fall into the handes of the liuing God, whome they contemned.

Oh how terrible a spectacle is it, to behold a grieuous sinner dye! I doe verily belieue, if the liuing cold discerne what hapneth within them a litle before they be caried away vnto their torments, that we should see most strange conuersions of many, who now liue without feare, or thinking of any care, perteyning vnto the next world. But this fauour is graunted but to few, nor haue we cause to demaund such priuiledges, as *Abraham* answered the Glutton that requested some messenger might be sent downe to admonish his brothers who were liuing : for *Abraham* bid them reade of *Moyses* & the propehts: as much as to say; you
must

must belieue what you reade in the
Scriptures, and not expect new. reuelations. The same do I desire the
reader, that he consider well, and
liue in such sort that he may dy like
a iust man in the most sweet peace
of God.

The consideration of the death of the Iust.
Chap. 10.

ALL the eloquence of the
world will come short, worthily to expresse the death of a iust
man. There is no riches, magnani-
mity, nor consolatiõ in this world,
that may admit any degree of comparison with the state of him who
dieth in the grace of Iesus Christ
our Lord. For admit we knew no
more of the death of a good man,
but onely this differéce, that when
the Potentates, and boisterous Spirits of this world, do tremble to

O   depart

departe hence; he who is in Gods
fauour resteth quiet, and peace-
able, and consequently God hath
as tender care of him according to
our vsual speech, as of the apple
of his eye, & he is naturalized into
the most pretious adoption of the
Sonnes of God, and made capable
of all the priuiledges which are in
due proportion allotted vnto so
happy a filiation : this I say, alone
would rise vnto so inestimable a
good, that all the treasures of the
world would seeme misery in
regard of this.

And from this happynes little
or nothing is to be detracted, albeit
a good man when he dyeth should
to vs seeme to endure great discomfort, and horrour of death. For if
he be truly the child of God, and
heyre of eternall life, of which
he is presently to take possession,
what importeth all the assaults of
the

the Diuells made agaynst him ?
what hurt can the frightings of the
Diuells do vnto him, whose soule
is resigned into the hands of God ?
Certainly, the infinite bounty of
God doth so sweetly order all
thinges with his seruants that appeare to be thus afflicted, that out
of anciét hystories, or fró later acci-
déts that haue byn noted in diuers
seruants of God, especially among
the reformed Orders, we can col-
lect no other thing, but that in the
middest of these molestations of
the Diuell, they haue byn vsually
visited, much recreated, and most
admirably comforted from heauen. So that the doubtfull speaches
which many tymes they vttered,
should rather seeme obiections of
the Diuell (and the frights of the
Diuell obtruded, rather an exercise of their fortitude) then any
diminution of their courage. For

in the middest of those seeming desolations, those who be about thē,
who haue liued well, do vsually
heare wordes of most firme confidence in Gods mercy, and most a-
matorious aspirations, full of most
tēder affections of the loue of God
to proceed from them.

Now, if their soules were de-
pressed with feare, & deiected with
the horrour of death, how could
their harts be so eleuated with so
diuine aspirations? And it is not to
be expected that euery good man
should dye after one methode. For
some who haue all the dayes of
their life practised extreme mortifications, may before their death be
visited with reuelations, which
will so sweeten the acerbity of the
circumstances of death, as they may
appeare heere to hauea taft of their
future ioyes, as S. *Gregory* relateth
many such. Others haue not thefe
ioyfull

ioyfull reuelations, but are left to
themselues to be molested with the
horrour of death, to giue them occafion to practise the actes of fortitude, of hope, of the loue of God,
becaufe Vertue is perfected in infirmity : and although the fenfe of
feare is not altogeather taken from
them, yet fecret ftrength is infufed
by God, that they may couragiou-
fly vanquifh feare, with the confidence in God, to the greater merit of him that lyeth a dying, much
edification of the beholders, & the
eternall glory of Gods holy name.
For there is no doubt to be made,
but that God will euer be faithfull
to thofe who ferue him, and in the
tyme of their greateft need, will
comfort them abundantly, far beyond that which we fee or thinke,
confidering the order of his fweeteft
prouidence : & this his correfpondence is moft neceffary at their

O 3 houre

houre of death; that euen as there be some reprobates, vnto whome vpon their death-bed the torments of hell are presented, so are there some elect, vnto whome it pleaseth God to communicate heauenly consolations, euen vpon their bed, where they haue consummated their holy life, with such patience, such resignation, so much hope, so much loue of God.

Now let the Reader thinke with himselfe what sense shall the soule of a good man feele, when it findeth herselfe so much fauoured and comforted by her Lord, whom she hath serued? What will she thinke when the houre is come, when Iesus Christ her Lord will say vnto her : Come my Beloued I will place my throne in thee: that is, I will sit in thee as in a throne of my Maiesty. What excessiue ioy will it be when she heareth her Sa-

uiour speake to her hart those mel-
lifluous and comfortable wordes:
Be not afraid my spouse, for I haue
made choice of thee from eternity,
& no power shall preuayle against
thee. Thou hast searched after me,
& loued me with all thy strength,
and I will presently attract thee to
me, and thou shalt fully enioy the
chiefe good, for the which thou
hast laboured so much, and fought
so lawfully.

  These be the consolations a iust
man hath, when he passeth out of
this life. Oh what a happines will
it be to serue Iesus hartily, this short
space of our life, that fadeth away
like a shadow! Oh how is this verity knowne, and confessed at the
death of such an one! Blessed is
that soule, that in that houre hath
the testimony of a good conscience,
and the confirmation of the works
of iustice. It is a perfect felicity that

a life paſſed ouer full of good
Works, humble Obedience, Apo-
ſtolicall Pouerty , pure Charity ,
feruent prayer, rigorous mortification, and practice of other vertues,
ſhould finiſh with right corefpondence of the Sonne of God . A iuſt
man when he dyes may remember
all that he hath done in his life, and
his iuſtice will cry Victory, victory . Then it will be proued true,
that Dauid ſayd : The iuſtices of
God do make the hart ioyfull. And
ſo not only in ancient tymes , but
in theſe latter dayes, I haue known
ſome ſeruants of God haue dyed
with that peace of mind, and ſecu-
ty of hope, as if they had receyued
frō Ieſus Chriſt, as a man may ſay,
ſome letters Pattents , of eternall
ſaluation , ſigned with his owne
hand.

This is ſo pretious a Iewell , ſo
ſo be defired & purchafed , as there
is

is no man so blind and senseles but
will confesse, that there is neyther
riches, greatnes, nor pleasure in this
world as may any way be compared heerewith , although a man
might enioy all the Kingdomes of
the world for a hundred thousand
yeare. And whē that instant comes
when the soule leaueth the body ,
she shall heare her Iudge with a
most louely gesture repeate those
words of the Canticles : *Arise, make*
hast my loue, my doue, my spouse ; the
winter is now past, the rayne is gone, the
stormes of mortality are ended : As if he
would say, Arise merily, be not a-
frayd my sweetest loue, my purest
doue, repose thee in thy wished-
nesse: most beautiful Spouse I will
now vnite thee in the bed of my
purest delights : Thou shalt haue
no more watchings, fastings, teares, temptations, or persecution :
now it is tyme that thou receaue
                    O 5   the

the reward which thou hast long
fought and expected : therefore
come, I will crowne thee, I will
giue my felfe vnto thee, as the right
meed thou haft merited.

And fince no humane wordes
can expreffe the thoufand part of
the fecret ioyes that fuch a foule
conceyueth, it is fit I fhould grow
filent, and only aske this queftion
of the Reader, whether peraduenture God haue not pleafed inwardly to communicate vnto him
fome touch of that fenfe which I
am no way able to explayne, by
meanes of his pious and attentiue
confideration of what he hath read.
For this bufineffe is not to be paffed ouer fleightly by him who wil
expect fo vnfpeakable mercyes.
Wherfore it is fitting he fhould earneftly defire to fuffer fome paynes,
be vifited with fickenes, be tried by
temptations, & all other forts of patience:

tience : for all these will quickely
haue an end , and he will reioyce
at hart when he shall dye; and will
neuer ceafe to sing the mercyes of
God, when he shall heare the Lord
of the Family commaund his faith-
ful steward to call al his workemē,
to pay them euery one their due
reward .

The confideration of the Iudgements of God. Chap. 11.

THOSE things which the
Scripture speakes of the iudgment of God, are so terrible, as may
well caufe a man who is but fmal-
ly deuout , to tremble very much :
but confidering that the elect haue
efcaped the terrour of the vniuer-
fal iudgemēt, being quitted in their
particuler iudgement; it will follow that a mans whole good dependeth how he paffeth his firft
    O 6   parti-

particuler iudgment . Therfore the
beſt Counſell, and fitteſt for Chriſtian prudence is, for a man to prepare himſelfe for his particuler
Iudgement, and alwayes in his life
to conſider what account he is to
make at that time. But who is able
to thinke, ſpeake , or write of the
ſtrict rigour of that examination ?
and although no man will be able
ſufficiently to expreſſe the ſame ,
yet piety exhorteth me to ſay ſom-
thing for the profit of the reader .
And therefore being requiſite I
ſhould ſay ſomething , I will lay
for my foundation the infinite hatred that God beareth agaynſt ſin ,
which is ſo extreme, and beyond
the compaſſe of our imagination,
that a man had need be aſſiſted by
the particuler grace of God , to
write thereof in any fit proportion : and therefore leauing this
point, vnto the wiſer conſideration
of

of the Reader, I will say no more,
but that sin, in oposition vnto the
purity of God, is so abhominable,
that it must needes prouoke him
vnto great indignation.

Moreouer I suppose that a voluntary veniall sinne, not only in
the piercing sight of God, but also
in the iudgement of a pious spirituall man, is more foule then any
leaper, or noysome thing, then the
most rotten and corrupted carcasse
that euer was beheld on earth; and
that to commit willingly but one
veniall sinne, is a greater infamy
and disgrace, then all the shame
that any worldly iustice can put vs
vnto, as the Deuines, without all
doubt, do conclude. Wherfore if
one veniall sinne so much displea-
seth God, what then is like to befall to that soule, that shall appeare
before God with one mortall sin?
Nay what may be expected if she
be

be all befpotted with many moft
deteftable mortall finnes ? It were
an excellent thing if a man cold
compaffe this in his cogitatiō,how
the purity of God will abhorre all
finne. To prepare a man vnto this
deepe conceyt, i would with him
to confider , what a horrour and a-
uerfion of mind he on a foden will
find in himfelfe, if he do efpy an v-
gly Serpent,or Dragon which feemeth to him to dart fire from his
eyes, nofe, and mouth . I thinke
he cannot deny, but that the ap-
prehenfion of feare will welnygh
ftrike him dead: and he will turne
away his face that he may not behold it,and he would be very glad
if any body cold kill it, and bury it
where he might neuer fee it.

Such extreme auerfiō God doth
beare agaynft finne. And although
we cannot properly fay , that the
Diuine nature is fubiect vnto fuch
impref-

impreſſions, **or apprehenſions** of
teare, or horrour of his owne part;
yet expreſſing the nature of one
mortall ſinne, we may imagine,
that if God could be capable of mu-
tation, the ſinne might vrge him
vnto ſuch paſſions. But although
in his nature he be immutable, yet
he hath expreſſed both in the old
and new Teſtament the infinite
diſlike and deteſtation he conceyueth agaynſt ſinne, and there is no
need I ſhould cite many examples
when one may ſuffice. For Luci-
fer was the moſt beautyfull and louely creature that euer God created; but he no ſooner ſinned, but he
was conuerted into the moſt vgly
and odious ſhape that can be ima-
gined, and God did ſo deteſt him as
he caſt him like a thunderbolt out
of heauen : euen ſo the ſoule that in
innocency is moſt amiable, com-
mitting but one mortall ſinne, be-
com-

commeth so odious in the sight of
God, that (if we may vse so vn-
seemely words) it is to turne the
stomake of God from looking on
her with any patience, and confe-
quently ought to make vs to tremble, when we thinke therof.

Wherfore a sinner ought before
hand to consider, in what sort the
Iustice of God will handle him, if
he appeare before the diuine face
in so vgly a manner. But this feare
must needs much increase, if we
(besides his most iust indignation)
do also ponder his strict manner in
examining the faulty, becaule he
doth obserue the actions of men so
curiously, that he will find out
sinne in their deedes which themselues least suspected, or rather
thought they had done well. Who
may not feare to enter before the
iudgement of Almighty God, since
it is not written in vayne, that
which

which *Dauid* fayth *Pfal. 74.* When
I fhall take time, I will iudge very
Iuftice it felie: meaning, Time is
mine, for I am Eternity it felfe, but
I haue lent men a Tyme in the
world, that they may haue free
Will to do good or euill, but it
fhall not alwayes be fo, but I will
reuoke my tyme when I fee caufe,
and will call them to fo ftrict a
reckoning, & fo iuft, wherin thofe
thinges which men ouerfaw in
themfelues with their carnall eyes,
my cleare fight will finde, euen to
iudge them worthy of punifhmét,
efpecially côfidering that they fhal
render account vnto me, nor only
of the offences which they haue
committed, but alfo for omitting
to do many thinges, which they
might, & ought to haue done.

If this be fo, who hath not moft
iuft caufe to feare to enter in iudgment of almighty God? Peraduenture

ture some few may answer almighty God, that actually they haue not comitted many offences. But who is able to say that the good deedes he did are so free from spot, or corruption, either of intention, or circumstance, as God may finde no fault therin? And if in this point also some should be found who may haue the confidence to tel the iudge that he directed his good deedes with as pure an intention, and obserued all those circumstances which he thought were necessary; then what will they be able to answere when God shall demaund account of them of diuers thinges they haue omitted to do, which they should haue done, nor did not thinke of then, being bound to consider the; and therfore diuers good men do in themselues descerne that their best deedes they study to doe, are so full of imperfections, that if
they

they fhould haue no ftricter iudge
then themfelues to paffe vpõ them,
they would fincerely cenfure them
as impure, and fit to be purged by
fire.

For let any man tell me, who is
he that recites his Office with that
attenſion, and reuerence as is fit to
fpeake vnto the Maiefty of God?
What man doth communicat with
that purity of foule , & application
of his mĩnde as is due to fo high &
Diuine a miftery ? Who is fo wary
in his wordes that doth not fome
tymes fpeake vayne or harmefull
words? Now if thefe workes in the
proper iudgment of him that doth
them be culpable, for the imperfections which they themfelues difcerne in them , what foulnes will
God find who will fearch thé with
a more curious eye? Surely he will
fay, that he can not deny but the
eyes of God will difcouer more
                          imper-

imperfections in those workes, which man wil thinke are Iust, but yet there is no great cause of feare, because he is free frō mortall sinne, although he haue committed a few veniall sinnes, which wil not prouoke Gods anger so much.

But let me aske of him that sayth so, how doth he know they be not mortall sinnes? For if he be obliged vnder payne of mortall sinne, to performe many of those workes which he holdeth good workes, how is he sure he hath fully discharged his obligatiō to God, since by his own cōfession they are imperfectly done? When a Priest sayeth his office whereunto he is obliged, is he certayne he hath cōmitted no mortal negligēce? When one confesseth his mortall sinnes which he is bound to doe likewise vnder mortall sinne, who knowes he hath omitted no necessary diligence

gence in examining his conscience, and hath that full purpose to forsake sinninge , that he may be worthy to be receaued into the fauour of God? And admit we might attayne vnto any certitude in these thinges, who is certayne he is free from all secret mortall sinne , that perchance he hath not taken sufficient care to search it out in himselfe, and to do pennance for the same ?

Besides, there be many dutyes to be performed to our neighbours vnder payne of mortall sinne : As for example , who knoweth if he be behinde in no duty towards his Children, with his seruants , with his creditours ? Oh how subtile are the examinatiõs of God in all such thinges : Peraduenture you may finde many a Iudge, Aduocate, Curate , or Prince, who in their own conceites hold themselues vpright,

that

that when God shall come to sift
them, may be damned for some
mortall sinnes, for not rendering
due iustice vnto their neighbours
according to Christian equity. The
more that I doe enter into considere-
ration of the iudgment of God, the
more playne it doth appeare vnto
me, that there are very few, who
without Gods great mercy will
be found to dye in fit state of saluation. For if a man had need of such
circumspection to be a iust man, &
ordinarily men take so litle care,
how can I be of any other opinion?

Heere I humbly beseech the
Reader, that to performe his duty to Iesus Christ, and for the loue
of his owne soule, he will first
iudge himselfe, before he come to
be iudged by the Maiesty of God,
and that he will not leane to such
reasons or arguments, which are
not

not very secure in a matter of that importance, wherin the least errour may do him so much haime. It seemeth strange to me, that they who haue least goodnes in them, should liue without feare, since those who are most illumined by God, liue alwayes in feare, according vnto the saying, *Blessed is that man who is alwayes fearefull, for he that liueth without feare cannot be iustifyed.* For both these proceed from more or lesse light of the soule, which naturally we discerne dayly. For one purblind looketh round about himselfe, but seeth not many spots in his apparell, which a man of a cleerer sight may easily discerne.

And for this cause, many who in the whole course of their life I haue knowne to be reputed very good men, and Priestes in their last dayes, and some of 80. yeares of age, haue entred to be Nouices in
some

fome orders of Religions, that in thofe lateft dayes, when they ftill expected death, they might moft exactly fpend their time in purifying of their confcience , and to prepare themfelues againft their iudgement before God; wherby they haue much profited their own foules , and infinitely encouraged thofe who were yonger to practice their examples. The time heere is fhort, we may be fodenly called on; wherfore let no man ftand on the idle opinion of the world , but procure to liue in fuch fort that he may confidently-prefent himfelfe before the iudgement of his Iudge Iefus Chrift the Sonne of God.

Of the confideration of the ftate of Hell.
Chap. 12.

ONE of the moft admirable, or rather moft Horrible things

in

in this life, is, that wheras euery
Chriſtian by the certitude of his
fayth knoweth, that at this houre
whē they read this, there are many
wicked men do actually ſuffer the
torments of hell which will laſt e-
ternally ; diuers I ſay, of them doe
notwithſtāding liue iuſt after that
manner now as the others did liue
before, that now burne in eternall
flames. In ſuch ſort if one ſhould
aske them, what they thinke of
thoſe works which ordinarily they
doe: they are like to anſwere, they
know full wel that they do deſerue
eternall torment. And ſome are
ſuch fooles : as they will ſo ſay in
ſport, and neuer take further care
to turne vnto God, or ſeeke remedy for themſelues in tyme. Nay
that which is moſt hartily to be lamented, is, that they frame to their
owne imaginatiō that the paines
of hell are eaſy to be borne, apting

P   them

them vnto their owne hardnes of hart and stupidity, that they seeme to want little of being no Christians. To such there is no more to be sayd, but that the Diuell hath blinded their iudgements by their most brutish appetites.

But now to speake vnto such who in a Catholik sense côfesse the paynes of hell to be most terrible, I demaund of thé what they meane? For is it possible for them to giue any credit vnto Gods truth, & yet liue as they do? For they ought to consider their soules were created for to enioy God the eternal good, and that by liuing as they do, they do depriue theselues of that chiefe good, which the Deuines call *Pœna Damni*, payne of Losse. Which priuation of the sight or vision of God we shall endure for euer. But supposing those damned Spirits who in their creation were Intellectual

Ange-

Angelicall natures, might haue any hope to regaine the moſt beautifull viſiõ of God which they haue iuſt-ly loſt, what thinke you wold they do? Nay what paynes would they not moſt patiently endure , that they might behold that moſt pure light , and bright-ſhining face of God , to loue, and ſerue that infi-nite ſuauity, & Diuine beauty?

Oh, what a groſſe errour are men in! Oh how do the Sonns of *Adam* deceaue themſelues of ſo a-miable a good, by immoderate vſe of the vayne externall toyes of this world! But ſome few ſpirituall men (who liuing corporally in the earth , mentally keep conuerſation in Heauen) belieue and know that the priuation of the viſion of God, & fruition of his moſt louely coũ-tenance is the greateſt puniſhment far exceeding all other torments.

But the reaſon why carnall & ſen-

fuall men do not know to frame
the conceit of the excessiuenes of
this payne (to be debarred for euer
from the glorious vision of God)
proceedeth from hēce, that hauing
(by an ill habit) lost the sense of all
spirituall consolation, they wish
still rather to wallow in the myre
of their obscenity, which is the
thing that will depriue thē frō beholding the glorious and pure face
of God; therfore it is fitter to talke
to them of a grosser subiect, to wit
of the payne of the sense, of which
they haue more feeling, & therfore
is liker to terrify them. And first I
will begin with the corporall fire,
because it must needes be that a sinner (who loueth so vnmeasurably
the ease of his body) will easily apprehend what a mischiefe it must
be to be thrown into the fire, there
to scald eternally. He knoweth by
practice, that if his bed be not easily

ly made, he cannot rest one night
in the same, without complaining
with great impatience of it. He re-
mébreth that although in the space
of one moneth he haue committed
many mortall sins, the least wherof were inough to deserue eternall
damnation, yet he will iudge it
intollerable, if his Confessor thold
enioyne him to fast one whole
day, or to pray but one houre vpon
his knees. He knowes if his shooes
do but pinch his feet, how he will
curse and sweare, and finally he
seeketh withall labour & diligence
to liue in ease and auoyd all paine:
How then will he endure to lye
naked perpetually in the scorching
flames of hell-fire? what wil he do?
what will he say?

Peraduenture all the storyes of
hell are but meere fables? Sure they
are but witty inuentions to mooue
one to pitty? They are not verities

of our Catholike fayth: what meaneth this brutish infenfibility in a sinner , that professing Christian Fayth, he liueth like a beast, more like a mad man , then a reasonable creature ? Yet if this continuall torment of hell might expire after the reuolutiõ of many years, or worlds of years, neither the hardnes of hart, nor the blindnes of a sinner would not be so intollerable : but since he knoweth there wil be no remedy , but that it will continue for euer, it seemeth that he is ouerdrunke with the delight of sinne, that he is become besotted like a beast without reason. For he is a most stupide creature, that for pleasing his appetite in a moment , will aduenture to suffer most raging payne for euer .

If there were a Bird that were to drinke dry the water that the Ocean conteyneth, by returning but
once

once in a hundred yeares, and then
drinke but one drop at that tyme,
and so vntill all that great sea were
exhausted; this might appeare some
hope of releasement : because it is
not only true, but most manifest ,
that all those innumerable millions of worlds , which passeth all
the art of Mathematicall computation, in the tyme that a Bird might
so consume all that water, would
seeme nothing in comparison of
that which is to be suffered in eternity , after that long tyme expired.
And it is most certayne , that the
least grayne of the finest sand hath
a more equall proportion with the
most spacious Empyriall heauen,
then the continuáce of those Millions of worlds with the perpetuall
paines of hell . Therfore what can
one say, but ōly be astonished at the
foolery of a sinner? But peraduenture it were better to say litue, or to

P 4   be

be silent, and to deplore the vnfortunate loss of those who runne the
way of wilfull perdition, and make
great hast to precipitate themselues
into the lake of torments .

It appeareth to me, that Iesus-
Christ our Lord doth continually
cry out vnto a sinner , speaking
thus vnto his hart by his mercifull
inspirations : *Whither goest thou, vn-*
gratefull man? why doest thou so furiou-
sly runne in the large way that leadeth vn-
to euerlasting payne ? Is it possible thou
shouldest be so desperate as to take no pit-
ty on thy selfe ? Stay thy steeps a while,
consider the end of this thy licentiousnes :
looke backe into thy selfe, & seeke to saue
thy soule. For certainly there is no
sinner but he somtimes seeleth this
counsell to be giuen him , in the
midst of his most carelesse courses,
by meanes wherof Gods iustice is
manifested when a sinner vseth his
own weapons vpon himselfe, whē
he

he is thus obdurate againſt God his
callings, and alwayes ſtrikes his
heeles agaynſt the pricke of his
owne conſcience, vntill he pierce
himſelfe to death; ſinning ſtill
with impudent wilfulnes, & infernall preſumption.

But what will he ſay when he
is caſt into Hel-fire amidſt the Diuels in vgly darknes; when he ſhall
feele the hůgry worme of his conſcience, that ſhall euer be gnawing
on him, as long as God ſhall be
God? with what barking & how-
ling will he reuile his owne madnes, that would not forbeare a
vaine delight of the world to imbrace the Croſſe of Chriſt? It is a
fearefull thing to be puniſhed with
ſo many ſeuerall ſorts of torments,
as a man can hardly nominate
without exceeding horrour. For
euen as Sinners haue offended God
particularly by all their members,

P 5   and

and in all their senses: So God hath ordeyned that they shall suffer punishment in the whole, & in euery member, and sense, answerable vnto iustice.

There therfore shall the wantō and lasciuious eyes be intertayned with vgly shapes of Diuells. The Hearing shall be cloyed with confused clamours & howlings of the damned that shall ring in his eares. The Smelling shal be infested with intollerable stenches of pestiferous sauous of that nasty place. The Tast shall be disgusted with loathsome meats, & distended with rauenous hunger, and vnquenchable thirst. The Touching shall be offended with vgly toades, and filthy vermine crauling and gnawing euery where. The whole body tortured with vnsupportable heat and cold. The imagination shall be tormented with all these present mischiefs.

The

The memory ſhall be excruciated
with calling to mind the idle delights paſt, which were cauſes of
this neuer-ceaſing payne. The vnderſtanding ſhall be perplexed by
repreſenting the good things that
are loſt, and the euills which will
euer poſſeſſe them. All the miſeries
in this life commonly come ſing-
ly. Some hath a payne in his head,
another in his eye, another in his
eares, another at his ſtomake, other
in his belly, & in ſome one limme;
and yet we ſee how one vſeth to
cōplayne if he ſpend but one night
without ſleep, being hindred by
ſome particuler payne.

But let vs imagine what oddes
would be if a man had ech of theſe
particuler paynes in euery lymme,
how inſupportable would it be?
what ſight cold moue more com-
paſſion? Certainly there is no man
ſo ſtony-harted that could endure

P 6

to behold a dog that seemed to be
in that anguish, but in compassion
of its extreme payne, would cause
the dog rather out right to be killed, then to permit him thus to be
plúged with payne in ech limme:
& I confesse, that the apprehension, during my writing, of this
state of the damned, doth much
perplex me; especially when I có-
sider, not how many may heeraf-
ter fall into this miserable state, but
how many millions me thinkes, I
see roaring in the middst of those
flames without hope of any deli-
uerance: yet as grieuous as this present cogitation is to me, I humbly
craue of Almighty God, that it may
neuer dopart out of my thoughts;
because during such a speculation,
there is no man willingly will offend God; since it is a terrible thing
to deserue so fearefull a iudgement.

Oh what a grieuous sight will
                                    it

it be at the day of the last vniuersall iudgement, to see so many nations of Creatures to be cast out from the shining face of the iust Iudge, with an eternall excommunication, neuer to be reuoked, or absolued? What a terrour will it be to see Diuels and men go downe togeather into that eternall prison, with infallible certitude that God wil neuer shew the least mercy to them, from the heauy sentence which he hath thundered out against them? Wherfore most mercifull Sonne of God, illuminate my eyes, and the sight of all sinners, that we may remember of what importance it is to serue thee heere, that we may be deliuered from the torments that are prepared for those vessels of thy wrath, that will not obey thee in the tyme of thy mercy.

of.

Of the confideration of the ioyes of
heauen. Chap. 13.

IT is moft certaine that neuer eye
hath feene , nor eare heard , nor
the hart of any man can conceiue
the greatnes , the confolation , the
aboundance of that fingular goodnes,which our Lord God hath prepared for thofe that doe loue his
nfinit goodnes . Yet it is good to
:hinke of it , and to treate in what
ort we can , of that moft happy
:ftate, which is the patrimony of
he Children of God ; to the end
hat our frailty may be comforted
with the hope of fo ineftimable
:onfolation, to defpife the falfe ap-
:earing tranfitory vanityes . There
s no doubt but the fonnes of *Adam*
do loue their owne commodity, &
that they who are good among thẽ
are wonderfully attracted with
that

that reward, that doth sweeten all
the bitternes, and doth make easy
all the labours of this life. Neyther
is it to be doubted of, but when a
man that hath any goodnes in him
doth confider, that for one act of
piety which he doth in the grace
of God, he shall receiue an eternall
reward; although that one worke
be perfected in a short time, yet he
will not sit downe there, but remembring the reward is so aboun-
dant, he likewise will striue to doe
more workes of that merit, that he
may seeme in some sort the more
worthily to deferue the same.

There is no such relation set
out by those who haue lately dif-
couered the West Indies, as is by
them who haue set forth, but in
humane prayse, the glory of heauen, which transcendes all humane
Oratory : Yet we see euery day
what strong effects it produceth in
the

the mindes of earthly men , that it
enforceth thé couragiously to hazard so many dangers by sea and
land, as were hardly credible, if e-
uery day did not affoard vs true
knowledge of it . Men heard only
that their was found great quan-
tity of gold and siluer, which are in
deed the Idols that still the world
adores,and only for this, they willingly indure so many great diffi-
culties; they leaue their father, and
mother, and acquaintance of friendes, the cōmodities of their owne
howse wherwith they are acco-
stumed, only with answering , It
may be they may returne home a-
gaine rich , and respected by those
of the world.

The imagination of gold is so
strong in their mindes, who are
created to despyse gold,and transitory riches , and to pretend and af-
pire vnto the only good which is
                                    able

able to satisfy the desires of men.
Therfore is it likely, that he who
will ponder the infinite riches of
that Citty of God that the citizens
doe there enioy, will take lesse
paynes then those others for the riches of the earth. I sayd lesse, because if they should take infinitely
more paynes, their labour will be
most aboundantly recompenced.
But for that consideration, is the
gate, by which the desires of eternall goods do enter into the soule:
let vs enter into consideratiõ therof somewhat proportionable vnto
mans insufficiency, ascending hig-
her by the light of fayth, then we
can clime by the helpe of humane
reason.

And first, let the reader imagine
what first befalleth a soule that shal
be discharged out of Purgatory, or
(if it be one of that few which neuer touch Purgatory) newly deliuered

uered from the Prifon of this body,
or this region of death, and fhall in
a moment enter into that gulfe of
the fpatious Ocean of diuinity, and
of the inenarrable delights of God?
Who is able fufficiently to expreffe the firft entrance of this Citty, where in an inftant fhalbe dif-
couered vnto the foule the infinite
beauty & delightes of the heauenly Paradife. But to conceiue fome
litle part of the whole deepeft fecrets, let the Reader fuppofe that
the foule of a good man (that hath
eyther byn purified in the fire of
Purgatory, or immediatly paffed
from the body to Heauen) flieth
with fuch a fpeed vnto our Lord,
who is his proper Center, as no
Eagle can make fpeed to purfue her
prey fhe feeketh after; and being let
loofefrom a cage of mifery, doth
like vnto the doue, that finding no
place to reft on in earth, flye with
alacrity

alacrity, to repose her selfe in the
Arke of *Noe.*

The soule that goeth from the
scorching flames of Purgatory,
mouteth with a most earnest lon-
ging to find her true cooling, and
when she entreth into that sea of
fresh and most pure waters, shee
drencheth her selfe deepe with a
desire to satiate her quenchles thirst
of loue, & there she reposeth with
an inward most sweet and secure
assurance, neuer to be depriued of
her loue whome shee possesseth.
Oh Happy lot, oh rich possession
that filleth brimme-full the empty
soule! Oh quiet Peace, that the
daughter of Sion, the spouse of the
only Sonne of God shall euer enioy! What louing wordes will the
enamoured Soule vtter vnto her
Creatour, & now her honoured
Lord, who so familiarly doth cō-
municate himselfe vnto her? Oh
                            my

my long defired good, fought by many labours, I haue now firmed thee vnto me with al my ftrength. I will neuer be feparated more frō thee; thou art all my refrefhment, my repofe, and my fweeteft life. Now I feare no more aduerfityes, becaufe I poffeffe thee who art the profound center of my ardent loue.

Thefe affections will the foule expreffe, that is naturalized to enioy the priuileges of heauenly Ierufalem. Now what pen is able to explicate, what mutual correfpondence will paffe from her Lord, who is all Loue, and hath receiued his deereft Efpoufe with in his clofeft imbracings, how wil he clafpe her, how will he infufe himfelfe into her, with what vnfpeakable fweetnes will he vtter fuch like wordes: Make ioy with me my deereft, inioy without feare of feparation thy chiefe good thou haft

so

so long desired with all thy hart.
Possesse me wholy, I am all thine.
Inioy (my Choice) the pleasant
fruits of Paradise, & feed thy selfe
vpon my beauty without satiety.

But why do I frame wordes,
since all words will come short to
expresse the least part of the im-
mense sweetnes of our Lord, that
glorifieth himselfe in rewarding
aboundantly the soule of the Iust,
which is vnto him a most sweet
fruite of his redeeming of vs, and
of his precious bloud which he
shed for vs. Certainely this is a secret kept from the eyes of mortall
men, that none can know but he
who receiueth it. Behold how I
am set vp in the very Porch, wheie
the soule entreth into the house of
God, which passeth all the eloqué-
ce and vnderstanding of man. But
if we consider the feast that all the
happy Cittizens of that place do
cele-

celebrate to congratulat that soule
(which they al loue as wel as their
owne) at its first coming to raigne
with them, I thinke I should smell
the sweet & fragrant odour of their
charity, & behold the swift streame
of that floud of ioy, which comfor-
teth the whole citty of God . Oh
with what imbracings , what pure
vnions , what tender speaches , do
they entertaine their new compa-
nion of eternall saluation! Oh how
do they singe the victories of that
soule, that ouercame the world ,
death , and Hell , and wonne the
kingdome of heauen by violence,
and gained vnto her selfe a perpetuall florishing life !

It would be of great importance, if men would consider the
reward which doth corresponde
vnto the workes of iustice. I know
not why they forget it . Surely it
would not procure any irksomnes,

or

or giue them any such distaste, as in penance they labour to auoyd. Certainely if they would spare themselues a little time, to ponder their future felicity, they would not giue theselues euer to the loue of temporall thinges, or haue their harts so hardned, and insensible of matters pertaining vnto God; but being allured with the beauty of heauen, they would giue themselues vnto the study of piety, with a most admirable change of their course of life. And discoursing with themselues of the felicity of glorified bodyes, it is likely (that by liuely contemplation of bodies that are configured with the body of our Sauiour Iesus Christe) they would be moued vnto the loue of their owne bodyes, being loth to be depriued of that cleare beauty which in the state of immortality they shall be endued with.

And

And becaufe my fenfes do faile me to expreffe the glory of this place, I will eafe my fpirits with fetting before the Reader a liuely defcription which S. *Auguftine* maketh in one of his meditations in thefe wordes : O life prepared for his frendes, bleffed life, fecure life, quiet, beautifull, cleane, chafte; moft holy life, which knoweth no death, no anguifh, no labour, no griefe, no anxiety, no corruption, no perturbation, no change or alteration; a life full of all dignity, where there is no enemy to feare, no delight watinge, where loue is perfect, euerlafting day, one minde in all; where euery one beholdeth the face of God, where they need no other repaft to feed on but the liuely fruition of his countenance; where a vertuous Knight being once arriued vnto thofe Quires of Angells, and his Head crowned with

with garlands of glory, doth alwayes sing vnto Gods glory, some
of the Canticles of *Sion*.

Blessed, thrice blessed shall be
my soule, if hauing passed my pere-
grination, I may deserue to see thy
glory, the beauty, the walls, the
gates, the streets of that Citty, the
Pallaces of those glorious Citty-
zens, the Omnipotent King in his
Maiesticall throne: the stones of the
walls are all precious, the gates are
emblished with pure Oriétal perle,
the streets paued with fine gold,
wherin neuer ceaseth to ring thy
prayses; the houses wrought with
Mosaicall worke, intertained with
Saphir, wherin no vncleane thing
can enter, no man dwell who is
not pure; sweet, and neate be the
delights of our Mother *Ierusalem*.
There is no such thing felt in thee
as heere we suffer, all is far different
in thee, from our miserable life

Q   heere

heere. In thee is neyther night, darknes, or any change of times. The light that shineth continually in thee, is neyther of lampes, or Moone, or bright starres, but God of God; & the light that proceedeth from his light, is the light that imparteth light vnto all. And the King of Kings sitteth in the midst of them, inclosed with all his faithfull seruants.

The Angels there do make most pleasing harmony: there the fraternity of the inhabitats reioyce kindly togeather; there euery one louingly welcommeth the pilgrims who come out from this world; There sit in order the prophets, the glorious bench of the Apostles, the Inuincible army of Martyrs, the Reuerend Conuent of true & Regious Confessours, the pure Virgins who in their weake Sex made the fortitude of men to blush, in
their

their vanquishing the enticings
of worldly pleasures : There are
yong men & yong women who
gaue example of grauity, and constancy to their Elders : There the
prety Lambes that escaped frō the
rauenous wolues, and the snares &
gynnes of this life, sport & playto-
geather; al their ioyes are equal, althogh there be different degrees of
glory ; there raignes charity in the
highest perfectiō, because God is in
them all, whome they all do behold , with whose loue they doe
all burne, they are all replenished ;
and in louing him, they perpetually prayse him, their prayses en-
kindle their loues , as wind doth
lighten fire, and the fire of loue in-
flaming thē, they neuer are weary
in glorifying him.

Oh happy , and thrice happy
shall I be, when deliuered out of
the prison of this little body, God

may

may make me worthy to heare the songes of that celestiall harmony, turned in the right Key of the high prayse of the eternall Monarch of all nations that are comprehended in that noble Citty of celestiall Ierusalem. But most happy shall I be when admitted among the quires of that Chappell, it will come to my turne to intone my *Alleluya* in prayse of my King, my Lord, my God, and behould him in his glory, as he hath promised when he sayd: Father this is my only and firme desire, that all those whome thou hast bestowed on me may liue with me, and be eye witnesses of the clarity that I had with thee before the creation of the world. Thus far goeth S. Augustine.

Now let the Reader ruminate with himselfe what a happy day will that be, that shall call in at your House, when casting of the

gar-

garment of mortality by the help
of death , you shall be reuested
with immortality, and in that paſſage , wherein others do tremble ,
you shall beginne to hold vp your
head , becauſe your Redemption
is at hand . *Saint Ierome* writing to
the Virgin *Euſtochium* , vſeth theſe
words: *Go forth* (ſayth he) *a little out
of the priſon of this body, and lying at the
gate of this tabernacle, ſet before your eyes
the reward of your preſent trauells. Ah!
were me; what a day will that be , when
the Sacred Virgin* MARY, *accompanyed
with a proceſſion of Virgins, ſhall meet &
receyue you ? When our Lord thy Spouſe
with all his Saints, ſhall encounter you,
ſaying: Ariſe my loue, my fayreſt, my
doue, make haſt, winter is now paſt, the
ſtormes are ceaſed, and the ſpring doth
bring flowers heere in our land ? But ſur-
paſſing will the ioy be of thy ſoule, when it
ſhall be preſented before the throne of the
Bleſſed Trinity, lead by the holy Angells;*
                                        but

Q 3

but *especially conducted by your Angell Guardian, vnto whose protection you were alwayes committed: when they shal relate your good workes done, your Croßes patiently endured, your labours constantly performed for the loue of God.*

S. *Luke* relateth, that whē the Holy Almes-giuer *Tabitha* dyed, all the Widdowes & poore people came round about S. *Peter* the Apostle, shewing vnto him their apparell that she had giuen them, by whose importunity the Apostle being mooued, prayed vnto God for that charitable woman, and by his prayers she was restored to life: euen so, when these holy Spirits before the diuine Consistory, shall display your charityes, your prayers, your fastings, the innocency of your life, your putting vp iniuries, your patience in affliction, your temperance in pleasures, with all the other good works which you
haue

haue done ; with what abundance
of ioy wil you be repleni∫hed? But
beyond all ioyes, this will euen ∫o
ouercome you, that being now in
the hauen of ∫ecurity , you may reflect backe vpon your dangerous
nauigation now pa∫∫ed , and ∫hall
di∫couer the rocks , the ∫helfes , the
Pirates that you e∫caped to be ∫o
many , that you will be enforced
to ∫ing that ver∫e of *Dauid* : *Vnle∫∫e*
God had protected me, it had byn a great
hazard , but my ∫oule had dwelt in Hell;
E∫pecially when from thence you
∫hall di∫couer the infinite number
of ∫innes that are committed dayly , & the multitude of ∫oules who
daily de∫cend into Hell, & ∫hal remember that God protected you a-
mong ∫o many thou∫ands , & hath
called you to this happy ∫tate. Your
∫oule would melt for ioy if it were
po∫∫ible. Oh how plea∫ant will the
ripe fruits of vertue there ta∫t, & be

cordiall

cordiall to the ftomake , whofe
greene budds were fo bitter on the
tongue heere, & feemed fo hard of
digeftion . Thefe ioyes are fo great
as it may feeme pride , & prefumption , to couet fo great matter : but
no man can liue for euer if he doe
not earneftly defire to enioy God ,
in whofe cleare vifion all thefe are
found .

Oh yee generatiõ of men, Children of *Adam*, who can thus blinde
you & deceaue you but your felues?
Oh yee ftrayed fheep, this is your
fold, returne hither, if you will not
be deuoured by the wolfe . Oh yee
fooles, why do you fuffer your felues to loofe fo infinite a good , for
fo fmall paynes taking ? If Croffes
be requifite to bring one hither, all
yee troubles of the world I inuite
you, come fall vpon me ? powre
downe vpon me all your forrowes
labours, ficknes , afflictions, iniu-
                                    ries

ries, infamies; let all dishonest creatures combine agaynst me, let me
be made a by-word of them all, &
a scorne of the world, that I may
at my death ascend vnto that glorious company, who are beautified
with such glory. Go to therefore
thou foolish Louer of the world,
seeke after Tytles, Honours, build
howses, and Pallaces, enlarge thy
Lands, and Patrimony, command
realmes, and worldes: for all these
thou shalt neuer be so great, as the
least seruant of God, which receyueth at his handes more then the
whole world can affoard, & shall
inioy it for euer. Thou with thy
Pompe, & Riches shalt be buryed
in hell with the Rich-Glutton,
when the poore seruant of God
shall be placed with *Lazarus*, in *A-*
brahams bosome.

Q 5

A TABLE

OF THE

CONTENTS.

of

Q 6   sinnes,

sinnes, that God at our death may be a milde Iudge vnto vs. Chap. 8. pag. 58.

The seauenth Precept, is to purge mans hart of the vanityes of this world, least he diuert his thoughts from those thinges, which will be necessary for his soule, at the tyme of his death. Chap. 9. pag. 66.

The eight Precept, is not to engage himselfe into too many businesse, least they distract his mind at his death for that they are not finished. Chap. 10. pag. 75.

The ninth Precept, is to exercise those acts of vertue as are most necessary for the houre of death. Chap. 11. pag. 82.

The tenth Precept, is to resist contagiously temptations, least the soule at the houre of death be ouercome therwith. Chap. 12. pag. 88.

The eleauenth Precept, is to appropriate some little tyme to consider the Agony of Death, doing some acts of Vertue, to obtayne patience, and conformity with

The

The second Part of the *Arte of dying well*; wherein is handled, the preparation fit to be vsed when one is neere vnto death.

THE *first Precept, concerning what a man should do at the first beginning of his sicknes.* Chap. 1. pag. 127.

The *second precept, concerning what must be done about the disposing of our temporall goods.* Chap. 2. pag. 135.

The *third Precept, what one ought to do, when his sickeneße doth increase.* Chap. 3. pag. 141.

The *fourth precept, of the due receyuing his last Viaticum, and the Sacrament of Extreme Vnction.* Chap. 4. pag. 146.

The *fifth Precept, what the sickeman must do, when he draweth nigh to dye.*

The

The third Part of the Art to dye well: Wherin is treated of diuers sorts of deaths, and the sundry accidents thereof.

FINIS.